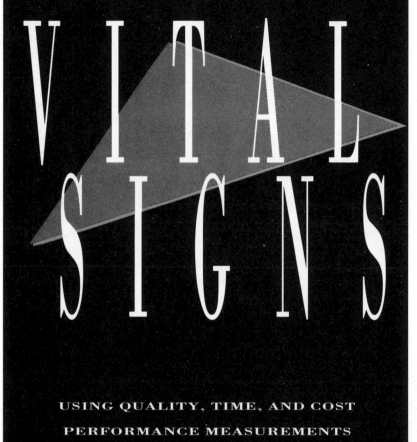

VITAL SIGNS

USING QUALITY, TIME, AND COST
PERFORMANCE MEASUREMENTS
TO CHART YOUR COMPANY'S FUTURE

STEVEN M. HRONEC
ARTHUR ANDERSEN & CO.

amacom

American Management Association
New York • Atlanta • Boston • Chicago • Kansas City • San Francisco
Washington, D.C. • Brussels • Toronto • Mexico City

This publication is designed to provide accurate and authoritative information in regard to the subject matter covered. It is sold with the understanding that the publisher is not engaged in rendering legal, accounting, or other professional service. If legal advice or other expert assistance is required, the services of a competent professional person should be sought.

Library of Congress Cataloging-in-Publication Data

Hronec, Steven M.
    Vital signs: using quality, time, and cost performance measurements
    to chart your company's future/Steven M. Hronec.
        p.   cm.
    ISBN 0-8144-5073-3
    1. Industrial productivity —Measurement.   2. Performance.
  I. Title
  HD56.25.H76 1993   92-43095
  658.5' 03—dc20   CIP

Printing number

10 9 8 7 6 5 4 3 2 1

TABLE OF CONTENTS

I decided to write this book for a simple reason: The way companies conduct business—the way they deliver their products and services to customers—has changed. And it's changed a lot.

The world has changed from the power being with the manufacturer and supplier to the power being with the customer. And this trend will continue to intensify. Organizations are adapting to this change using many different concepts.

One concept involves focusing on the customer and looking at a business from the outside in rather than the inside out. This concept has many names—Total Quality Management, Total Quality Control, Continuous Improvement—all with the idea of understanding the customer and changing the business processes to align them with customer wants. New organizational structures encourage simpler, more immediate communication. New human resource concepts—such as empowerment and teamwork—support a more participative management style. New production and delivery technologies—such as Just-In-Time, time compression, and quick response—put a premium on speed and first-time quality in all a company's processes. And new environmental factors—rapid technology advances, transportation improvements, increased competition globally, and changing regulations—add both challenge and complexity to the idea of competitive advantage.

The last thing most companies change is performance measurement. But this should be the **first**. Performance measurement—the right kind of measures—can drive change throughout an organization. As countless studies have shown, people act as they are measured. To change a performance measurement system is to change how people understand their contribution to the corporate vision, mission, and strategy.

But what are right measures? This, too, has changed. To match today's new structures, management styles, and processes, performance measures must have a few critical qualities: they must be simple, close to activities, actionable, and helpful in supporting management strategies.

In many client companies, I have seen a lack of appropriate performance measurement act as a barrier to change and improvement. And I have seen this lack lay to waste the best efforts of everyone to implement changes in structure or process. Without performance measurement, improvement cannot be meaningful; it cannot last.

This book is my attempt to help executives in every industry update and expand their understanding of **why** performance measurement is so important and **how** they can develop and implement a new system of measurement, one that is focused on the right things, in the right place, at the right time.

As the "vital signs" in an organization, performance measures can—and should—help a company achieve competitive advantage and then move beyond that to Quantum Performance.

Steven M. Hronec
Arthur Andersen & Co.

LOOK FOR THESE VITAL SIGNS
ON THE FIRST PAGE OF EACH
CHAPTER:

■ DEFINITIONS

● BENEFITS

▲ RISKS

ACKNOWLEDGMENTS

The writing of **Vital Signs** has been a team effort, and I would like to thank all who have contributed to the process. I thank Richard Measelle, Managing Partner of Arthur Andersen; James Hooton, Managing Partner of Audit and Business Advisory Services; David Phillips, Managing Partner of Industry Initiative; and Robert Hiebeler, Managing Director of Global Best Practices Initiative, for their enthusiastic reception and support of this project.

Particular thanks are due to the following for contributing, reviewing, and critiquing substantial portions of this book, and especially for keeping me focused: Reid Dalton, Leng Eng, Holbrook Hankinson, Maggie Hoag, and Shelley Lloyd. Thanks are also due to the following reviewers and contributors at Arthur Andersen: George Dunne, Mort Egol, Steven Hunt, Jean Kennedy, Richard Kreutzfeldt, Chak Lau, Tony Livernois, Chuck Marx, Thomas White, and Debbie Wood.

I also would like to thank the people at Arthur Andersen, AMACOM, and Monaco/Viola who helped with the design, production, and marketing, including Mary Angert, Becky Bercini, Pat Charpentier, Kristine Martin, Mark Monaco, Bob Viola, and Andrew Welling.

But most of all I would like to thank Kathryn, Steven, Mark, Rebecca, and Rachel for their patience and support throughout the development of this book.

Dedicated to all the clients of Arthur Andersen, without whom none of this would be possible.

Steven M. Hronec

1

QUANTUM

PERFORMANCE

■ **DEFINITION**

Performance measures are the "vital signs" of an organization. They quantify how well the activities within a process or the outputs of a process achieve a specified goal.

● **BENEFITS**

The "vital signs" tell people what and how they're doing as part of the whole. They communicate what's important throughout the organization: strategy from top management **down,** process results from lower levels **up,** and control and improvement **within** processes.

▲ **RISKS**

Only with a consistent view of the "vital signs" can everyone work toward implementing the strategy, achieving the goals, and improving the organization.

One day, while waiting to meet with the CEO of a large manufacturing company, I looked around the reception area. Displayed prominently on the wall was this statement: "This organization provides products and services which consistently meet or exceed standards set by our customers, on time and at the lowest cost." That's a good mission statement, I thought. It shows that the company focuses on customers and wants its products and services to meet and exceed customer expectations. At the same time, the company considers the service dimension ("on time") and the cost dimension ("at the lowest cost").

When I entered the CEO's office, I complimented him on the mission statement. It was obviously very important to the company, I said, because I had noticed it in several places as I walked from the reception area to the CEO's office. It was on the wall in his office, too.

Then I asked, "But how could you know?" He looked at me, not understanding the question. I elaborated, "As the CEO of a large multinational organization, what report do you get on a periodic basis—not daily, but quarterly, monthly, semimonthly, whenever—to tell you what your customers' standards are and whether you're meeting or exceeding those standards?"

He looked at me but didn't say anything. I continued, "How about 'on time'? If time is an important measure, and it's part of your mission statement or strategy statement, what report do you, as CEO of this company, get on a periodic basis to tell you whether you are delivering your products and services to your customers on time? Or how about 'lowest cost'? 'Lowest' is comparative. You surely must get some sort of report about your competitors' costs—a report you can believe." At this point he looked—or rather, glared—at me, and we continued our conversation.

The CEO had to admit that, although his mission statement was powerful, there was no way that he knew whether that mission was deployed throughout the organization. He had no way of knowing whether people in the organization were working toward that mission.

This scenario is not unusual. Management spends a lot of time developing mission statements, but often gets diverted from the details of developing a set of performance measures. Why? Because the development of performance measures is very difficult. It requires balancing stakeholder interests, understanding customers (both internal and external) and their wants, and identifying company processes. This simply cannot be done during an executive weekend retreat. In many companies, the top executives do not even have basic facts.

Here's the point I was trying to make to the CEO: If goals such as cost, quality, and time are important enough to be in the mission statement of an organization, then there ought

Management spends a lot of time developing mission statements, but often gets diverted from the details of developing a set of performance measures.

3

Performance measures should be derived from the mission statement.

to be a way of determining whether those goals are being achieved. In other words, performance measures should be derived from the mission statement. The CEO should be getting a periodic report that tells whether the company is achieving its goals. That's what performance measures are: vital signs that answer the question, "How do you know?"

After we completed our conversation, the CEO took the first step toward a top-down, cascading use of performance measures to link the organization to the mission. He started the process of determining **what** to measure and **where** to measure in the organization.

Performance measures should drive the strategy throughout the organization so that all people in the organization understand what the strategy is and how their work and their performance are linked to that overall strategy.

Between the corporate mission statement and performance measures is **strategy:** the plan for achieving the mission. Performance measures should drive the strategy throughout the organization so that all people in the organization understand what the strategy is and how their work and their performance are linked to that overall strategy.

Performance measures can answer the "how do you know" question. But most companies don't measure the right things in the right ways. Simply put, the traditional measures used by organizations —earnings per share, return on investment, actual to budget, labor efficiencies, variance against standards, inventory levels, machine utilization— aren't appropriate. They aren't really wrong; they're just incomplete. Each of these measures looks at only one part of an issue, often a very small part. And when each measure is examined separately, the organization may focus on the wrong things.

So, why use performance measures? Before answering that, we must address another question: What are performance measures? That's often where the trouble begins. Companies do not have a clear understanding of what performance measures are, much less how to use them.

VITAL SIGNS

Performance measures are the "vital signs" of an organization. They tell the people in an organization what and how they're doing and whether they're functioning as part of the whole. They communicate what's important throughout the organization: strategy from top management downward through the organization, process results from lower levels upward to top management, and control and improvement within a process.

But communication within organizations is difficult. In fact, it often gives rise to inappropriate expectations and actions. Why? Because if people don't use the same definitions, follow the same rules, or have the same boundaries, they can't communicate effectively.

This communication problem is evident in writings about quality and in programs designed to "embed quality" in companies. In one department,

Performance measures are the "vital signs" of an organization.

for example, quality may mean "zero defects"; in another, it may mean "speed to market." As a result, the actions of these departments—perhaps excessive inspections on one hand and expediting orders on the other—are at odds. Each department might perform well according to its own definition of quality and using its own measures, but the performance is poor and, at the very least, excessively costly. Although using the same words, people are not communicating with one another.

When performance measures are linked to the strategy of the organization, everyone uses the same definitions. This common understanding means that everyone follows the same rules and works within the same boundaries. With this consistent view of the organization's vital signs, everyone can work toward implementing the strategy, achieving the goals, and improving the organization.

The first rule of performance measurement is this: Achieve 100 percent understanding throughout the company on terms and objectives. To that end, the definitions here and throughout this book provide a necessary foundation for common understanding. They provide everyone the same rule sets or boundaries.

A **performance measure** is a quantification of how well the activities within a process or the outputs of a process achieve a specified goal. Performance measures must be developed from the top down in an organization and must link the company's strategies, resources, and processes.

The first rule of performance measurement is this: Achieve 100 percent understanding throughout the company on terms and objectives.

A performance measure is a quantification of how well the activities within a process or the outputs of a process achieve a specified goal.

Since correctly designed and implemented performance measures look at processes as well as outputs, they do more than identify problems. They also help everyone in a process anticipate and prevent problems.

Quantification is an important part of this definition. To measure something, dimensions, amounts, or capacity must be determined. Measurement requires the act of "measuring" and should be, therefore, reliable and consistent, with a basis in fact, not opinion or hunch or gut feel.

The judgments "good" and "fast" are not adequate performance measures. "Number of defects" or "time for order processing" are acceptable measures **if** they are actionable—that is, if the people performing the work can affect the output.

Example: Frederick W. Smith, chairman and CEO of Federal Express, has been quoted as saying, "We believe that service quality must be mathematically measured" (*Blueprints for Service Quality: The Federal Express Approach*, 1991). Fed Ex's quality goals are 100 percent customer satisfaction after each and every interaction and transaction, and 100 percent service performance on every package handled. The company uses a 12-item statistical quantification of customer satisfaction and service quality from the customer's viewpoint. The 12 items are tracked every day, both

individually and in total. Each of these items
is defined and communicated to employees.

*A process is a series of
activities designed to
produce a product
or service.*

A **process** is a series of activities designed
to produce a product or service. To measure
"activities," one must first understand the process
of which the activities are a part.

Results are important. We are not proposing to
eliminate the measurement of "results." If process
measures drive a company to improvement ("a
specified goal"), output measures keep score. One
type of measure without the other is only half the
picture. (See Figure 1.2 for a definition of **process**
and **output** measures.)

Ordering fast food is an example of a
familiar process.

1. Customer walks through door.
2. Customer waits in line.
3. Customer reviews and selects from menu.
4. Customer places order.
5. Counter person keys in order.
6. Customer pays for order.
7. Customer waits for food.
8. Customer receives order.
9. Customer takes order to a table or leaves
   the facility.

To determine performance measures for this
process, restaurant management first must
understand the customer's specified goal:
to have a quick, inexpensive, hot meal.
Therefore, the performance measures used

by the restaurant should be set around those goals and activities:

- How long do customers wait in line? If the lines are too long, the company should change its planning to add counter personnel.
- Is the food delivered hot? If the food sits too long, measures within the process inform everyone that the food is beyond its shelf-life and is no longer usable.
- Is the food competitively priced? Keeping an eye on the market enables a company to stay competitive.

The performance measurement system must link to the organizational strategy. The strategy of the organization should be broad and long term, and it should include the various stakeholders of an organization: customers, employees, shareholders, regulatory agencies, suppliers, and so forth.

BENEFITS OF PERFORMANCE MEASURES

FIRST BENEFIT: SATISFYING CUSTOMERS

As the vital signs of a company, performance measures can—and should—focus everyone on the company's single most important mission: customer satisfaction.

Customer satisfaction keeps a company in business. Without customer satisfaction, the company will lose market share to its competitors and will cease to exist. Without a continual drive toward customer satisfaction, the company will not know the product characteristics or service elements necessary to remain competitive based on market demand.

People behave as they are measured, and a company's performance measures reflect its real goals versus its image goals.

People behave as they are measured, and a company's performance measures reflect its **real** goals versus its **image** goals. A company might adopt "customer satisfaction" as its mission, tout it in the annual report, and post it in the reception lobby. But, if profits are the company's primary definition of success, employees will do everything necessary to meet financial objectives **first,** maybe at the expense of customer satisfaction.

Financial objectives are not inappropriate. The fault lies not in financial measures, per se, but in the fact that they are the overwhelming priority for most companies.

Performance measurement is really a balancing act.

Schlesinger and Heskett (1991) found a relationship between internal service quality, employee satisfaction, employee retention, external service quality, customer satisfaction, customer retention, and profit. See Figure 1.1. This research, along with our experience with clients, shows that performance measurement is really a balancing act. A company can't have an acceptable rate of return without satisfied customers, yet customer satisfaction alone is not sufficient insurance for long-term survival. That's why, although customer satisfaction may be the primary purpose of performance measurements,

it is not their **sole** objective—any more than profit is a company's **sole** purpose.

SECOND BENEFIT: MONITORING PROGRESS

As companies try to apply output performance measures—such as improved productivity or lower costs—to processes, they're often frustrated with the results for one simple reason: Management doesn't understand the company's processes.

The right performance measures make process improvement not just possible but continuous.

Yet, actual process improvement is a key to long-term performance. A company that can make a better product (that is, one more suited to customers' needs and wants), in less time for less cost, is bound to succeed. The right performance measures make process improvement not just possible but continuous.

An example of a performance measure that focuses on continuous process improvement is the tracking of the number of activities within a process. Over time, such a measure encourages the people in the process to keep decreasing the number of steps or activities in the process in order to increase its speed and, therefore, its flexibility.

Performance measures provide the information needed to focus on the best processes and allow comparisons between companies.

THIRD BENEFIT: BENCHMARKING PROCESSES AND ACTIVITIES

Performance measures make possible "management by facts." They should provide the information needed to focus on the best processes and allow comparisons between companies.

Best Practices is simply the best way to perform a process or an activity within a process. **Benchmarking** is a structured method of measuring processes and products against others. It's the metrics of Best Practices.

In one example of benchmarking and Best Practices, a U.S. electronics company seeks to improve its purchasing functions by talking with an automotive manufacturer to find out how that manufacturer decreased its ranks of suppliers and what measures it used to measure supplier performance.

FOURTH BENEFIT: DRIVING CHANGE

Why do so many companies spend dozens of days and thousands of dollars designing processes to implement their strategies, only to leave those designs in a binder gathering dust on a shelf? A strategy can carry the best intentions; a process design can hold the right answer. But without implementation, they are of no value. The right performance measures help organizations change successfully, because the right performance measures break down barriers and, in many cases, **prevent** barriers.

Performance measures facilitate communication within a process and throughout a whole organization. Yes, material usage and quality

The right performance measures help organizations change successfully.

13

must be accounted for, but this is only the first level of adequate performance measurement. In fact, most companies already have more than enough "numbers" attached to their processes (look at labor efficiency reporting in manufacturing, for example). But what about people? People make change happen, so people must be measured, too. The right performance measures help organizations change because they define and reward new behavior.

Research and experience have demonstrated that the most effective, least costly way to change human behavior is through measurement.

Research and experience have demonstrated that the most effective, least costly way to change human behavior is through measurement.

Example: Milliken & Company uses performance measures extensively to define good performance. As Tom Malone, president, says in his long-range presentation: "Teams that don't keep score are only practicing." The company has overall key performance measures that tie to the company's overall strategy of improving customer response. Each process has its own measures, defined and monitored by the people doing the work within the process. At the process level, the performance measures help the associates anticipate and prevent problems and continuously improve processes.

THE BEST
PERFORMANCE MEASURES

The best performance measures give balance
to the company's operations and are deployed
throughout the organization in a way that links
strategy to processes and processes to one another.
Recall the definition of performance measures:
the quantification of how well activities within
a process, or the outputs of a process, achieve
a specified goal.

PROCESS AND OUTPUT

There are two types of performance measures,
as shown in Figure 1.2:

Process performance measures monitor
the activities of a process and motivate
people within the process. In other words,
they control the process by allowing people
to anticipate and prevent problems. Some
examples are setup time, number of skills,
cycle time, and customer response time.
Physical or nonfinancial process measures
are common, particularly at lower levels
of the organization, where physical indicators
have more direct meaning.

Output performance measures report
the results of a process, often to management,
and are used to control resources. Output
measures can be financial or nonfinancial.
Some examples include net income, earnings
per share, customer satisfaction, and
organizational flexibility.

Quality can be achieved only if a company has the right balance of output and process measures—output measures to keep score and process measures to drive improvement.

CASCADING EFFECT

Performance measures link the mission, strategy, goals, and processes of the organization.

A process measure for one organizational unit can be an output measure for the next lower unit. Each level of an organization should support the processes of the next higher level. The result of this cascading effect is that performance measures link the mission, strategy, goals, and processes of the organization. Since this cascading effect starts at the top, management needs to tell employees at the lower levels what is important: The mission drives activities. In turn, only strategic information is reported up, thereby eliminating the unnecessary reporting that is so common today.

HORIZONTAL VIEW

Performance measures should reflect a horizontal view. The process of receiving an order, making a product, and delivering that product to a customer is not vertical; rather, the process flows horizontally across departments.

Performance measures such as lead time, flexibility, and customer service cannot be fulfilled by one department alone. Departments must work together to satisfy customer needs. Performance measures also must be horizontal, mimicking the processes themselves.

FIGURE 1.2
**PROCESS AND OUTPUT
PERFORMANCE MEASURES**

PROCESS MEASURES
- Report the activities of a process.
- Motivate the people and control the process.

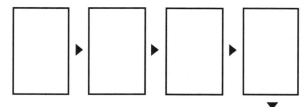

OUTPUT MEASURES
- Report the results of a process.
- Control resources and monitor results.

FAMILY OF MEASURES

There are three categories of performance measures:

- **Quality** quantifies the "goodness" of a product or service.
- **Time** quantifies the "goodness" of a process.
- **Cost** quantifies the economics of "goodness."

In each case, "goodness" is defined by the recipient or interested party. In the case of quality, it's primarily the customer; for time, it's primarily management; and for cost, it's the various stakeholders, including management and shareholders.

Focusing attention simultaneously on cost, quality, and time, a company can optimize the results of the processes—and can optimize the results of the whole organization.

By focusing attention simultaneously on cost, quality, and time, a company can optimize the results of the processes—and can optimize the results of the whole organization.

There also is a relationship among these three categories of performance measures. When customers receive a high-quality product—one that meets and exceeds their expectations—at a very reasonable or low cost, they are receiving high value. Therefore, the relationship between cost and quality is a "value" relationship to customers. When customers receive a high-quality product—one that meets and exceeds their expectations—very quickly, they believe they are receiving a high level of service. Correspondingly, the relationship between quality and time is a "service" relationship. These relationships are depicted in Figure 1.3.

FIGURE 1.3
FAMILY OF MEASURES

Companies need to optimize their value and service to customers continuously. World-class companies are going beyond "competitive advantage," because sometimes the performance of competitors is not remarkable or exemplary. If an individual company does not strive to overcome its competition **greatly**—to optimize **all** its resources and **all** its processes—it may be at a disadvantage in the future when its industry attracts new competition or the environment suddenly changes. In short, world-class companies are going beyond the status quo to focus on "quantum performance."

QUANTUM PERFORMANCE

Quantum performance is the level of achievement that optimizes the organization's value and service to its stakeholders.

Quantum performance is the level of achievement that optimizes the organization's value and service to its stakeholders. There are a lot of very important words in this short definition.

First is the concept of a "level" of achievement. Quantum performance is measurable. It means achieving specific levels as targeted and directed by top management and by their strategies. The goal is **overall** optimization as opposed to the optimization of only one factor, department, or function. Cost, quality, and time must be improved **simultaneously.**

Quantum performance addresses an organization's **value** and **service**—or the relationship of an organization's cost and quality to its customers and the relationship of an organization's quality and time to its customers. And the concept of customers should be expanded to include stakeholders—customers, employees, shareholders, regulators, environmentalists in some industries, and the different people and entities who have a stake in the outcome of an organization.

QUANTUM PERFORMANCE MEASUREMENT MATRIX

Once management accepts the family of measures—cost, quality, and time—it needs to understand how to use them throughout the organization. In their book *Improving Performance: How to Manage the White Space on the Organization Chart*, Geary Rummler and Alan Brache (1990) describe the three levels of deploying performance measures in an organization.

One level of performance is the **people**—those doing the activities and being directed by a set of performance measures. The second level of performance is the **process**—the series of activities that consume resources and provide a product to the company's customers, either internally or externally. The last level of performance described by Rummler and Brache is the **organization**—which encompasses the performance at the people and process levels. See Figure 1.4.

With the levels as a basis, we can devise a three-by-three matrix—a **Quantum Performance**

Quantum Performance Measurement Matrix shows the use of [performance] measures through the organization at the organization level, the process level, and the people level.

FIGURE 1.4
THE LEVELS OF PERFORMANCE
Adapted from Rummler and Brache (1990).
Used with the permission of Jossey-Bass, Inc.

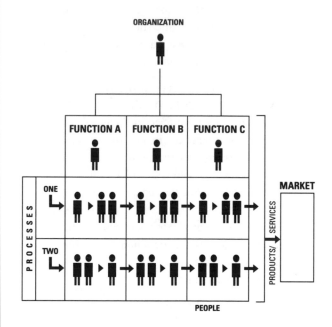

Measurement Matrix (the Matrix). As shown in Figure 1.5, the Matrix includes the family of performance measures of cost, quality, and time. It also shows the use of these measures through the organization at the organization level, the process level, and the people level. (The Matrix is discussed in detail in Chapter 2.)

QUANTUM PERFORMANCE MEASUREMENT MODEL

To determine the performance measures within each of the nine areas of the Matrix, management needs a process—a **Quantum Performance Measurement Model** (the Model). See Figure 1.6. This Model has many benefits. It provides a framework for performance measurements—a context to show where people are in the process of developing, implementing, and using performance measures. And, it allows and encourages communication during the process.

The Quantum Performance Measurement Model consists of four distinct elements.

The first element is **drivers.** The driver of performance measures, strategy, takes into account the leadership of the company, the stakeholders, and the Best Practices in the environment. (The environment includes competition, regulation, resource availability, market availability, and so forth.)

The second element of the Model is **enablers.** Enablers support the implementation of performance measures through **communication.**

Quantum Performance Measurement Model provides a framework for developing, implementing, and using performance measures and encourages communication during the process.

23

FIGURE 1.5
QUANTUM PERFORMANCE
MEASUREMENT MATRIX

QUANTUM PERFORMANCE		
VALUE		SERVICE
COST	QUALITY	TIME

(row labels: ORGANIZATION, PROCESS, PEOPLE)

FIGURE 1.6
QUANTUM PERFORMANCE
MEASUREMENT MODEL

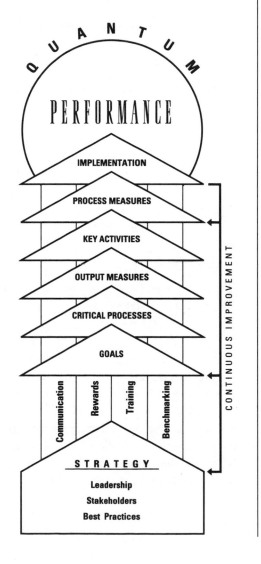

How can performance measures be communicated throughout the organization? Through **training.** How can an organization change the way people do things? Through **rewards.** How can Best Practices be used as targets in goal setting? Through **benchmarking.**

The third element of the Model is the *process itself.* The goals of the organization are driven by the strategy. Next, it is necessary to identify and understand the critical processes in the organization. Then output performance measures are deployed through the organization. Key activities are identified within those processes. Once that is done, the process performance measures can be developed to control and monitor key activities and all the performance measures can be implemented.

Performance measurement is a process, not an event.

The fourth element is ***continuous improvement.*** The Model provides feedback for continuous improvement, for the setting of new goals, and for the adjustment of strategy. The key point is this: Performance measurement is a **process,** not an event. The goal of the Model is to drive an organization to quantum performance—to develop performance measures focusing on cost, quality, and time that allow an organization to optimize its value and service to stakeholders. This Model may be used at **every** level, in **every** part of an organization. Each area needs its own strategy, its own goals, output measures, and so forth.

In the rest of this book, we will show you how to use the **Quantum Performance Measurement Matrix** and the **Quantum Performance Measurement Model** to develop performance measures that will support your efforts to achieve quantum performance— the optimization of your organization's or your department's value and service to its stakeholders.

THIS BOOK EXPLAINS HOW TO DEVELOP, IMPLEMENT, AND USE A PERFORMANCE MEASUREMENT SYSTEM THAT WORKS—A SYSTEM THAT LINKS ALL PROCESSES TO THE STRATEGY OF THE COMPANY, WHILE GIVING THE PEOPLE WHO *PERFORM* THE PROCESSES THE TOOLS TO IMPROVE THEM CONTINUOUSLY.

2 | THE QUANTUM PERFORMANCE MEASUREMENT MATRIX

■ **D E F I N I T I O N**

The Quantum Performance Measurement Matrix is a tool for balancing multiple measures (cost, quality, and time) across multiple levels (organization, processes, and people).

● **B E N E F I T S**

The Matrix allows management to start to understand and develop performance measures that balance value and service in a way that matches company-specific strategies, goals, and processes.

▲ **R I S K S**

Without the Matrix, a company risks a suboptimal view of how performance measures should complement the complexity of the organization.

Quantum Performance Measurement Matrix allow[s] management to understand and develop performance measures that balance cost, quality, and time.

The goal of the Quantum Performance Measurement Matrix (Figure 2.1) is to allow management to understand and develop performance measures that balance cost, quality, and time. The following high-level overview of the Matrix does not cover all possible performance measures. These are not **absolute** performance measures; but the Matrix does allow management to start understanding and developing performance measures that balance value and service in a way that matches company-specific strategies, goals, and processes.

As mentioned in Chapter 1, one level of performance is the organization. Traditionally, companies are functionally segmented: marketing, engineering, sales, manufacturing, research, finance, and so forth. Measurement at this level is output-oriented and after the fact.

Yet, although companies are organized functionally, they provide services to their customers horizontally—not through marketing, not through manufacturing, not specifically through finance. They provide services to their customers **across** functional boundaries. Customers are served through processes. That's the second level of the organization: the processes that cut across the functional boundaries. Measurement at this level is process-oriented and intermediate.

The third level of performance is within the organization, within the processes, within the functions: **people.** Performance measurement at this level is actionable and immediate.

FIGURE 2.1
QUANTUM PERFORMANCE
MEASUREMENT MATRIX (DETAILED)

QUANTUM PERFORMANCE		
VALUE		**SERVICE**
COST	QUALITY	TIME
Financial Operational Strategic	Empathy Productivity Reliability Credibility Competence	Velocity Flexibility Responsiveness Resilience
Inputs Activities	Conformance Productivity	Velocity Flexibility
Compensation Development Motivation	Reliability Credibility Competence	Responsiveness Resilience

ORGANIZATION · PROCESS · PEOPLE (row labels)

Across the top of the matrix is the family of performance measures: cost, quality, and time (remember, cost and quality together equal "value"; quality and time together represent "service"). Along the side of the matrix are performance measures through the three levels. First, let's define each category:

Costs are the financial performance measures—the dollars spent on the people, processes, or organization. This category measures the economics of "goodness."

Quality is the way customers define it. From a performance measurement standpoint, quality means that the products or services meet and exceed the wants and expectations of the customers. This category measures the "goodness" of the product or service in the eyes of the customers—internal or external.

Time is a function of the speed of the organization. How fast can the organization be responsive to outside influences, either through customer orders, a change in competition, or a change in the environment? This category measures the "goodness" of the process.

It's also important to recognize that the Matrix allows for both process and output measures, which are defined by **how** the measurement is used: to report results or to improve the process (see Chapter 1).

The Matrix allows for both process and output measures, which are defined by how the measurement is used: to report results or to improve the process.

32

THE PEOPLE LEVEL

Since people and process measures roll up to the organization level, it makes sense to start at the primary point: the people level (Figure 2.2).

Quality: Let's start with people measures for quality, because quality is really what the customers want. In the Matrix, we have three types of people measures under quality: reliability, credibility, and competence. Reliability is "consistency of performance." Credibility is "trustworthiness." And competence is "possession of necessary skills and knowledge."

What are some examples of these performance measures? Reliability in a service environment could be performance to schedule—whether an individual meets his or her due dates. In manufacturing, it's often error rates. Credibility is a personal characteristic that's very important in the service industry, where many employees—the salespeople, the receptionist, the telephone operators— are in contact with external customers.

Many service industries have a wide range of personal characteristics they look for in employees. For example, banks train their tellers to present their image and have the personal characteristics of trustworthiness and believability.

The third type of quality performance measure for people is competence: the possession of skills. The depth of skills—how well someone does his or her job—can be measured both in service

FIGURE 2.2
**PERFORMANCE MEASURE
DESCRIPTIONS, DEFINITIONS,
AND EXAMPLES**

PEOPLE LEVEL

	DESCRIPTIONS	DEFINITIONS	EXAMPLES
COST	Compensation	Acquiring and deploying the skills of people	• Salary costs • Benefit costs
	Development	Training and education	• Training meetings • Seminars • Coaching • Mentoring
	Motivation	Encouraging people to continuously improve	• Sharing sessions • Reward/ Recognition programs
QUALITY	Reliability	Consistency of performance and dependability	• Performance to schedule or promise • Error rates
	Credibility	Trustworthiness, believability, and honesty	• Personal characteristics
	Competence	Possession of required skills and knowledge	• Skill level/ Proficiency • Certification
TIME	Responsiveness	Willingness and readiness of employees to provide prompt service	• Time to respond to questions, inquiries, etc.
	Resilience	Flexibility and positive attitude toward change	• Number of skills • Individual readiness to change • Number of suggestions submitted

and manufacturing, through proficiency tests and often through certifications.

Time: In the time column, at the people level, two typical measurements are responsiveness and resilience. Responsiveness is "willingness and readiness of an employee to provide prompt service." This is important in both manufacturing and service industries. For example, lots of companies are very concerned with how long telephones ring before they are answered or how quickly an employee can fulfill a request. These indicate responsiveness.

Resilience means flexibility—the "ability of employees to change." If people have more than one skill, they can change based on the varying demands of the customers. If people have more than one skill, they can do things better. And they can move from one project to another.

Many manufacturers, through their contracts with the unions or through their agreements with their employees, are encouraging their employees to be flexible. For example, they encourage employees to acquire additional skills through training courses and educational funding. And some companies, if a downturn forces management to shrink the work force, evaluate not by seniority, but on number of skills: Those with the most skills stay. In this case, people are encouraged to improve continuously, to broaden their range, and to improve their skill sets.

Likewise, service organizations have recognized that, because of the changing demands of their customers, the changing demands of the environment, or because of competition, it's important to have flexibility in the work force. These organizations are training their employees to have broader skills so they can adjust and react to change faster. And they are teaching skills and planning ways to increase them continuously.

Another example of resilience, in both service and manufacturing, is the number of suggestions that employees give to the organization. Companies that have very good suggestion policies and practices, and very good suggestion programs, change faster. Why? Because their employees are constantly looking for ways to improve the organization. An example is Milliken & Company, which has right now about 30 suggestions per employee per year. Even more amazing is that Milliken has implemented more than 80 percent of those suggestions. Milliken has benchmarked Toyota. (See Chapter 4 for a discussion of enablers and benchmarking.) The Toyota suggestion system generates 50 suggestions per employee per year. And Milliken is driving for that "Best Practice."

Cost: At the people level, cost includes compensation: salaries and benefits. It also includes training (How does one increase the skills of people?) and motivation (How does one encourage people to improve continuously?).

Now let's look at the interplay between the cost, quality, and time performance measures at the people level. If a company wants to increase resilience, it can do that in different ways: by training—that's developmental costs—or by hiring—that increases compensation costs. Because there are trade-offs, companies have to manage all three categories of performance measures simultaneously. What's important is that a company look at the big picture. How do performance measures link to the strategy of the organization? How do they help manage cost, quality, and time within the organization?

THE PROCESS LEVEL

Quality: Let's move up to the process level (Figure 2.3). For quality, consider two performance measures: conformance and productivity. Conformance is "effectiveness": Is the process doing the right things? Productivity is the "efficiency" of the process: Is the process doing the right things in the right way? Both of these are important in service and manufacturing environments.

Conformance shows whether the process meets the characteristics demanded by the customer. For that reason, it's equivalent to "quality." Productivity, on the other hand, is whether the process meets the operating needs of the company's management. Does it get the job done without waste or excessive cost? Productivity is just as appropriate a measurement in service processes as

FIGURE 2.3
PERFORMANCE MEASURE
DESCRIPTIONS, DEFINITIONS,
AND EXAMPLES

PROCESS LEVEL

	DESCRIPTIONS	DEFINITIONS	EXAMPLES
COST	Input	Cost of process inputs	• Raw materials • Capital costs
	Activities	Cost of performing a process activity	• Cost of vouchering • Cost of billing • Cost of preparing a blueprint
QUALITY	Conformance	Effectiveness of a process: usually an attribute performance measure of whether the output of a process meets and exceeds customer satisfaction	• Product/Service characteristics
	Productivity	Efficiency of a process: doing the right activities in the right way	• Units produced or processed per given input (e.g., rate per hour, number of attempts) • Process path length • Number of activities in a process
TIME	Velocity	Speed of delivery of the process output	• Cycle time
	Flexibility	Ability of the process to respond to varying demands	• Setup time • Multitask equipment

in manufacturing processes. The productivity measurement of process path length, for example, applies to paper flow such as that in a billing process, where an invoice can travel miles through buildings before it is sent to the customer. Redundancy is another sign of waste or cost. One service company checked its figures 12 times before releasing its bills, yet 50 percent of the bills went out with clerical errors. As companies become more and more productive, they're able to decrease the number of activities, decrease the process path, and increase productivity.

Time: Still at the process level, time has two types of performance measures: velocity and flexibility. Velocity is the "speed of the delivery"—how much time elapses from a customer order to product or service delivery. Flexibility is the "ability to change"—how the process can change to meet varying demands, either from the customer or from the environment.

Cycle time is very important to manufacturing and service companies. So is flexibility. In manufacturing, flexibility includes setup time for equipment. As setup time decreases, manufacturing lot sizes can be smaller; the company is able to change and adjust production levels very rapidly. In the service industry, flexibility is also important. An example might be software. How flexible is the software? How many tasks can be performed with the software?

Cost: The cost cell includes two types of costs, the first being inputs to the process. In manufacturing, that's simple: raw materials, supplies, capital costs, depreciation. In the service industry, input costs include people, depreciation, leases, light, heat, and power.

The second type of costs is activity costs. What is the cost of doing a specified activity? Companies have to answer that question from a cost-analysis standpoint to make informed decisions about product costing, make-buy, new plant locations, or product/service lines. The tool being used is activity-based costing (see Chapter 8), which assigns the cost of an activity to a product, a process, an output, or a make-buy decision, based on resource consumption.

THE ORGANIZATION LEVEL

An organization is made up of processes and people—people working within processes to meet customer wants and demands. In the Matrix, performance measures at the organization level are really the rollup of the performance measures at the people and process levels. At this point, they're output performance measures, but they address the same things. See Figure 2.4. Again, let's start with quality.

Quality: At the organization level, quality measures include empathy, productivity, reliability, credibility, and competence. Let's cover just a couple. Empathy is "individual attention." No more mass production. Every

FIGURE 2.4

PERFORMANCE MEASURE DESCRIPTIONS, DEFINITIONS, AND EXAMPLES

ORGANIZATION LEVEL

	DESCRIPTIONS	DEFINITIONS	EXAMPLES
COST	Financial	Historical financial information reported under external rules	• IRS • SEC
	Operational	Financial information used to run the business on a day-to-day basis	• Sales backlog • Sales • Cash balances
	Strategic	Financial analysis used to support long-term decisions	• Make/Buy analysis • Product cost analysis • Target cost analysis
QUALITY	Empathy	Individualized attention	• Customer satisfaction rating • Employee satisfaction rating
	Productivity	Organizational efficiency	• Sales per employee • Units produced within a time frame • Outputs divided by input
	Reliability	Consistent and dependable performance	• Product returns • Customer complaints
	Credibility	Stakeholders' perception of organization	• Image surveys • Public relations scores
	Competence	Skills required to perform	• Third-party certification • Client references
TIME	Velocity	Speed at which an organization delivers various outputs	• Order fulfillment cycle time • New product development time
	Flexibility	Ability of an organization to respond to varying demands	• Number of organizational levels and span of control
	Responsiveness	Ability and willingness to provide prompt service	• Time required to act on customer requests • Average time it takes to reach the person called
	Resilience	Flexibility and positive attitude toward change	• Organizational change readiness index • Number of suggestions implemented

customer is unique. How do companies know whether they have empathy? Through value surveys of external and internal customers. Do customers and employees think the company treats them as individuals? Companies with empathy have superior customer and employee satisfaction ratings.

Reliability, at the organization level, is "consistent and dependable performance." From a manufacturing standpoint, that's simple; it's often measured by the number of product returns or warranty costs. Most manufacturing companies capture and analyze customer complaints, either through toll-free numbers or surveys. Service organizations can do the same thing. Yet, most service organizations don't, because people within service organizations fear that complaints are their fault; they think they have failed the customer. This is a major weakness in a lot of service companies. Complaints should not be used as a judgment of employees, because the problem (the reason for the complaint) usually originates in company processes. If service companies are not capturing, analyzing, and identifying customer complaints, they are missing a major source of information from which they could improve their processes.

Credibility at the organization level is the "stakeholders' perception." There are many different performance measures at the organization level—such as image surveys, to name only one. An organization has to understand how it is viewed by **each** major stakeholder group, and the organization should measure how these different stakeholders perceive its credibility.

Time: Moving over to time now, organization-level measures include velocity, flexibility, responsiveness, and resilience. Let's spend a few minutes on these.

Velocity is the "speed" at which the organization delivers various outputs. How fast can the organization provide products? In the manufacturing environment, it's very important that new products be developed in a very short time frame. The faster a new product is developed, the easier and faster a company can react to changing customer demands. But that same shortened time frame is just as important in a service organization. If a service organization—an advertising agency, a professional services firm, or a financial institution—can decrease its speed to market in offering new service lines or new products, or in entering into new markets, it has a tremendous advantage.

Responsiveness is the "ability and willingness to provide prompt service." Tom Peters did a little test to gauge responsiveness at Federal Express. He called 27 times; service representatives answered after the first ring 26 times. The 27th time he let it ring five times, thought he misdialed, hung up, and tried again. The call was answered after the first ring. Responsiveness: Customers aren't going to wait. It's very important that companies provide prompt service.

The final time measure at this level is resilience. How positive is the organization's attitude toward change? This can be measured in various ways—through change readiness surveys, for example. Another interesting measure of resilience is the number of suggestions the company implements. At the people level, a performance measure might be the number of suggestions, but it's the organization's responsibility to use these suggestions. Companies that implement a high percentage of their people's suggestions are flexible—ready to change. Again, at Milliken, more than 80 percent of suggestions offered by associates are implemented; at Toyota, the percentage is even higher.

Cost: At the organization level, the company needs three types of cost measurements.

First, **financial**—the historical financial statements compiled according to external rule sets, generally accepted accounting principles, SEC rules and regulations, and so forth. These show what has happened to the organization from a historical financial perspective. This is often referred to as cost accounting.

Second, **operational**—the cost of running the business on a day-to-day basis. What is the cost of the processes or of the people, day in and day out? An example of operational cost information for manufacturing is sales backlog. For a service industry, it's daily cash balances or daily sales. Linking these cost measures to quality and time measures is often referred to as cost management.

Third, **strategic**—financial analysis used to support long-term decisions. This starts with the information from processes, the cost of activities adjusted for some environmental influences. It looks to the future and is used by manufacturers and service organizations for make-buy decisions, product cost analyses, and target cost analyses. Do we enter a new market? Do we develop a new product? From an organizational standpoint, cost rolls up from people and processes. This is often referred to as cost analysis. Chapter 7 deals with the development of cost performance measures at the organization level.

VITAL SIGNS

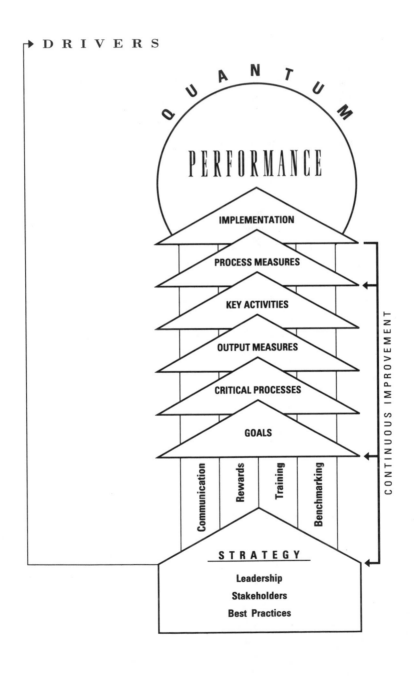

DRIVERS

QUANTUM

PERFORMANCE

IMPLEMENTATION

PROCESS MEASURES

KEY ACTIVITIES

OUTPUT MEASURES

CRITICAL PROCESSES

GOALS

Communication

Rewards

Training

Benchmarking

CONTINUOUS IMPROVEMENT

STRATEGY

Leadership

Stakeholders

Best Practices

3 | DRIVERS

■ **DEFINITION**

The Quantum Performance Measurement Model is a systematic, logical, coherent, and comprehensive approach for the development, implementation, and use of performance measures.

● **BENEFITS**

The Model starts with strategy, which derives from three sources: leadership, stakeholders, and Best Practices. Performance measures, done right, drive the company strategy down to every level and every process in the organization.

▲ **RISKS**

When developing performance measures, people can be limited by old paradigms: a functional organization structure, a financial view, and an "events-driven" focus.

The Quantum Performance Measurement Model (the Model) is a systematic, logical, coherent, and comprehensive approach for the development, implementation, and use of performance measures.

The Model starts with strategy, which cascades throughout an organization, and moves through performance measures, which keep the company focused on what's important.

Since any strategy includes a goal of quality, this chapter covers basic Total Quality Management (TQM) concepts before discussing the three sources, or drivers, of strategy: leadership, stakeholders, and Best Practices. Finally, strategy is developed within an environmental context, which is addressed later in this chapter.

QUALITY

The definition of quality keeps changing and expanding. As customers and stakeholders can get more, their expectations increase and companies must provide more. To define quality in such a way as to reflect a customer focus—and then to initiate and implement performance measures to match—moves beyond "parts produced per hour" or even "zero defects."

"Quality" is understanding, accepting, meeting, and exceeding customer needs, wants, and expectations, continuously.

Quality means different things to different people. In fact, only a few years ago, "quality" was defined as "meeting customer specifications, no more and no less." Today, "quality" is "understanding, accepting, meeting, and exceeding customer needs, wants, and expectations, continuously."

Understanding. More than just sending out surveys and questionnaires, "understanding" means working with customers to know their true wants and expectations. Understanding is an ongoing process, not a task or an activity.

Understanding can start with focus groups and progressive groups as well as one-on-one discussions with customers. Further understanding comes from forming cross-functional teams that include a variety of people, notably from marketing but also from production, R&D, etc. Working closely together, these teams enable the organization to understand the needs of everyone in the process, including the external customer.

As companies move down this path of ever-greater understanding, they can—and should—expand their customer focus to include their customers' customers. This higher level of understanding enables companies to "anticipate" their customers'—and their customers' customers'—needs, wants, and expectations. Anticipation is, after all, really a higher form of understanding.

Accepting. As companies understand their customers' wants and expectations, they often find out that many of the characteristics of their products and services are not valued by their customers. In addition, they learn about things their customers want, but that they haven't provided. Acceptance makes "quality" personal.

"Understanding" means working with customers to know their true wants and expectations…an ongoing process, not a task or an activity.

It's one thing to get the results of a survey or to hear the recommendations of a project team, but it's quite another for an individual to sit back and accept what is being said. It's a question of ego. Acceptance of feedback is difficult, as is acceptance of suggestions for improvement.

When told that customers complained of difficulty in opening cans of beer, the CEO of a major brewery said, "Our beer is the best. They'll find a way to get it out " (Zenger, 1992). Clearly, this is not a good example of "acceptance."

To improve acceptance, consider asking customers a few pointed questions:

- What do you need from us?
- What do you do with the product/service we give you?
- What are the gaps between what you need and what we give?

Meeting. To meet customers' wants and expectations, management must know what customers think they will be receiving (what performance characteristics a product will have, that service will be performed within a certain time frame, and so on).

It's necessary to distinguish between perceptions and expectations. Here is one common definition of quality:

$$\text{Customer Satisfaction} = \frac{\text{Customer Perception}}{\text{Customer Expectation}}$$

Expectation is what customers think they
will receive as they enter a relationship or
transaction. **Perception** is what customers think
they received as they exit the relationship or
transaction. In both cases, what's important
is what the customers think. This is where
the complexity lies, since there's often a gap
between what companies think they've sold
and what customers think they've bought and
also a gap between what companies think they
have delivered and what customers think they
have received.

One manufacturer, for example, was mystified
when a customer said some newly purchased
equipment was of poor quality—that it did
not perform to specifications. Through testing
on-site, the manufacturer found that the
equipment's performance actually exceeded the
claims in the company's marketing literature.
But further investigation uncovered the
problem: The sales force was overstating the
capabilities of the equipment and thereby
increasing customer expectations. It didn't
matter what the marketing material said
or even how the equipment tested. The key
was what the customers expected.

It's important for companies, as part of their
customer service or customer satisfaction
process, to manage both customer expectations
and perceptions. That includes developing
performance measures to make sure that all
communications to the customers before the

*It's important for
companies…to manage
customers' expectations
and perceptions [by]
developing performance
measures…on
communications that
set expectations
[and]…on customer
contact after the
transaction.*

51

transaction—that is, those communications that set expectations—are appropriate as a part of the long-term company strategy.

At the same time, it is important that companies manage customers' perceptions—that is, what occurs after the transaction or after the service. Companies should have performance measures in place that focus everyone's attention on customer contact after the transaction. These would include information calls from customers, service and warranty contacts—anything that affects customers' perceptions. Many times customers are not aware of all the characteristics and all the service elements of a product or transaction. The right performance measures for communication with customers are important in the management of customer perceptions.

Exceeding. Quality has more than one dimension. To truly satisfy customers, a company should at least "meet" expectations in all dimensions and "exceed" them in some.

The product and service characteristics that exceed customer expectations are those that, in the words of Dr. W. Edwards Deming (1991), make customers "rejoice in the relationship" with the provider of the product or service.

The definition of quality extends beyond a product's physical characteristics to its service or information dimensions. "Exceeding" is how and where true differentiation comes in. Exceeding customer expectations makes a company stand out in the field and creates switching costs. Customers are loyal to products and services that exceed their expectations.

But here's the catch. The more customers get, the more they want. Expectations increase over time, hence the need for a never-ending cycle of continuous improvement. In the 1980s, American car manufacturers did not make worse cars than they had 10 years before. In fact, the cars were better. But the Japanese cars were of such high quality that they altered expectations of U.S. customers, and thereby decreased their satisfaction with U.S. cars.

Example: Let's illustrate this point with a simple product: a ballpoint pen. Company A's pen is 5½ inches long and blue; it has a cap, weighs about half an ounce, and has enough ink to write 1,000 yards. If Company B makes a pen with the same physical characteristics, the two would meet customer expectations equally, and customers would have no switching costs in choosing between Pen A and Pen B. Only when Company A does something to improve its pen so that it exceeds expectations—makes it write 2,000 yards (product), delivers the pen anywhere in the world (service), or shows how to use the pen better (information)— will customers remain loyal.

CHANGING PARADIGMS
It's easy to define quality, but it's hard to understand it, because doing so requires that we change our rule sets, or **paradigms.** Joel

Barker (1992), who has popularized the term "paradigm" through his lectures and videos, has the following definition in his book, *Future Edge*:

> A paradigm is a set of rules and regulations (written or unwritten) that does two things: (1) it establishes or defines boundaries; and (2) it tells how to behave inside the boundaries in order to be successful.

There's a big difference between the traditional paradigm of quality—"meeting customer specifications"—and the new one—"meeting and exceeding expectations."

There's a big difference between the traditional paradigm of quality—"meeting customer specifications"—and the new one—"meeting and exceeding expectations." Joseph Juran (1992) calls the two paradigms "q" and "Q": "little quality" and "Big Quality."

"q" focuses narrowly on product features and functions—the traditional old-line manufacturing definition of quality. "Q" has a total-company perspective and includes all the people and activities that come together to meet and exceed customer expectations.

This difference is often one of the primary reasons for misunderstanding in organizations. Some people think about quality under the old view—or "q"—while others view quality under the new way of operating—"Q." (See Figure 3.2 for a comparison of "q" and "Q.")

FIGURE 3.2
QUALITY PARADIGMS

QUALITY PARADIGMS

q	Q
Inspect in quality	Build in Quality
Increased quality increases costs	Increased Quality decreases costs
Procedure-oriented	Process-oriented
Departmentally driven	Leadership-driven
Meet customer specifications	Meet and exeed customer expectations
Focus on shop floor/manufacturing	Holistic focus on entire organization
Second-person (quality is someone else's job)	First-person (Quality is my job)

Many people are limited by their old paradigms when they deal with performance measurement concepts.

Many people are limited by their old paradigms when they deal with performance measurement concepts. One is the functional structure: Individuals work within specific functions and are measured within those functions; these measures are often financial, such as budgets. It is very difficult for functionally oriented people to focus on processes and on the performance measures that would enable them to control and improve those processes.

A second outdated paradigm for performance measurement is the financial view, whether historical or budgetary. It is very difficult to break away from financial comparison—to use nonfinancial performance measures to report results or to improve processes.

A third old paradigm is that performance measures are event-driven. Because people find transactions important and interesting, they focus on this type of performance measure.

But continuous improvement occurs through the processes, so performance measures should focus on process improvement—not on events.

LEADERSHIP

It's important that leadership provide direction to the performance management system.

Since performance measures drive an organization, it's important that leadership provide direction to the performance management system. A company's leaders must say: "These goals are important to our strategy, and we want these measures to run the business." Six months or a year down the road, they still have to ask: "How are we doing? Is each measure still relevant?" The leadership of an organization must begin and nurture the Model. And the Model both requires and makes inevitable one thing: change.

The leadership need not wait until all the top officers of the company are together 100 percent. Five percent commitment from all levels makes change possible; the other 95 percent eventually go along as long as they are not aggressively antagonistic. In many organizations, 10 to 20 percent of the people may strongly resist change, but this will not prevent it, as long as there is leadership commitment.

What's important is that the change process be controlled; as management involvement and commitment change over time, the change process does too. One of the best ways of controlling change is through performance measures.

ABO Continuum[SM]

The ABO (Awareness, Buy-In, Ownership) Continuum[SM] gauges progress in the Model. In the beginning, no one executive has complete ownership of the new performance measures because no one person understands all their ramifications or implications. The ABO Continuum (see Figure 3.3) helps companies gauge management's commitment to performance

ABO Continuum is a service mark of Arthur Andersen & Co.

FIGURE 3.3
ABO CONTINUUM

AWARENESS ▶	BUY-IN ▶	OWNERSHIP
• Seeks to learn performance measurement issues	• Seeks guidance to act on performance measurement issues	• Seeks and assumes responsibility for performance measurement issues
• Commits time to understand	• Commits time and resources to be involved	• Recruits others to be involved
• Understands performance measurement concepts	• Uses performance measurement concepts	• Applies and teaches performance measurement concepts
• Is passively supportive of performance measurement efforts	• Is actively supportive of performance measurement efforts	• Initiates performance measurement efforts

measures and to the Model. This continuum was developed by looking at actions taken by leaders of top-performing companies.

Awareness: Executives know something important is happening, and they show interest in it. During the awareness stage, the leaders of a company seek to learn more about the family of performance measures, attend meetings to discuss the concepts of the new family of performance measures (see Chapters 1 and 2), and allow their paradigm of traditional performance measures to be challenged.

Buy-In: Executives move from awareness to a commitment to the Model. They begin to take personal responsibility for what's going on. They are willing to commit time, people, and money to the process in support of the organization. During the buy-in phase, leadership moves the organization to use the new family of performance measures, uses performance measures to drive strategy throughout the organization, and communicates the benefits of the new performance measures to other people in the organization.

Ownership: Executives become role models in the process and assume ultimate responsibility for performance measurement. Ownership comes when leaders assume responsibility for changing their own performance measures, challenge the performance measures in their areas of operations, and teach the concepts and help other areas adopt the new family of performance measures. Being role models, leaders recruit others through working with employees one to one or talking in informal settings.

The ABO Continuum operationalizes the fuzzy concept of "management commitment." "Management commitment" means moving through the awareness, buy-in, and ownership phases in a controlled manner, supported by performance measures that allow the company officers to know whether they have management commitment.

The ABO Continuum links to the family of performance measures discussed in Chapter 2. The awareness stage of the continuum is a measurement of the "competence" of leadership—leadership's possession of required skills and knowledge. The buy-in stage of the continuum is a measurement of the "resilience" of the leadership group—its flexibility and positive attitude towards change. Finally, the ownership stage of the continuum focuses on the personal characteristics of leadership—"credibility."

To move the leaders along the continuum, it's useful to involve them actively in collecting data by having them listen to external and internal stakeholders to develop strategy. Leaders must be able to balance the needs of all stakeholders. When the customer is Number One, many times employees feel they are Number Two. It's important that leaders take a multilevel, multi-interest view. As shown in Figure 3.3, executives move through stages. This takes time. The movement should be controlled and measured over time.

We have used the Executive Commitment Checklist shown in Figure 3.4 to determine where top executives are in accepting the new performance measures. We list the names of the executives under the first column on the chart and ask each to tell the group where they think they are. If all executives do not come to consensus on the rating, then the executive in question is asked to provide specific examples until the entire group comes to agreement.

STAKEHOLDERS

Stakeholders are individuals, groups, or organizations affected by the processes, products, or services of an organization. Today, companies are broadening the focus of their strategies beyond customers to all stakeholders; their wants and needs must be understood in order to optimize the value and service of an organization.

Stakeholders are individuals, groups, or organizations affected by the processes, products, or services of an organization.

Critical stakeholders include external customers, employees, stockholders and investors, governments, and various regulators—including environmental organizations. When developing strategy, management must identify the various stakeholder groups and also understand their expectations and wants. Most companies do not go through this process systematically.

One of the most important stakeholders of any company is its customers, defined as everyone who receives an output of a process:

FIGURE 3.4
**EXECUTIVE COMMITMENT
CHECKLIST**

E X E C U T I V E

AW**A**R**E**N**E**S**S**	**COMPETENCE**				
	Seeks to Learn				
	Commits Time to Understand				
	Understands Concepts				
	Gives Passive Support				
BU**Y** **I**N	**RESILIENCE**				
	Seeks Guidance				
	Commits Resources				
	Uses Concepts				
	Gives Active Support				
OW**N**E**R**S**H**I**P**	**CREDIBILITY**				
	Assumes Responsibility				
	Recruits Others				
	Applies/Teaches Concepts				
	Initiates Efforts				

External customers use the end product or service of the process but are not members of the organization that produced the product or service.

Internal customers (employees) are affected by the products or processes, but are within the company's organization. The internal customer is often the next person in a process or a person in the next process.

It's critically important that the goals and objectives of **internal** customers be consistent with those of the organization. If they aren't, they will inhibit the company from meeting—and exceeding—the wants and expectations of **external** customers. Too often, internal customers request or require specifications, services, or information that is not valued by the external customer.

It's critically important that the goals and objectives of internal customers be consistent with those of the organization.

Example: The external customer of a defense contractor was the government buying the product; the internal customer was the project director. Everyone in the manufacturing process focused on the next step in production. The project director made specification requests and requirements that were significantly tougher than those in the government contract. When asked why, he said, "to get it right." His arbitrary demands, based on distrust, cost the company a great deal in scrap and rework.

Why might an internal customer place "excessive" demands on an internal supplier process? For two reasons: because it puts him in a power position vis-á-vis the rest of the organization serving him and because he doesn't trust the previous process and overcompensates by building in a cushion.

Excessive paperwork can be a sign of inappropriate internal customer requests. A lot of people write and keep reports just in case the next person in the process might ask to see them—even if that person is not affected by them. "The boss wants them" is the explanation. Why? Often, a habit just to keep people busy.

Without customers, a company would go out of business. That's an obvious fact, but few companies actually make customer satisfaction a primary focus of their business despite slogans or mission statements that "put the customer first."

How do we know? Because only a handful have performance measures that focus on the customer. And since people act as they're measured, it stands to reason that an absence of measures directly related to customer satisfaction indicates a lack of companywide follow-though on that objective.

Perhaps this gap between action and words exists because customer focus is hard to maintain, given operating and financial pressures and the potentially conflicting interests of various stakeholders. In addition, it's hard to keep up with customer demand because that demand is consistently escalating: Customers want more than ever because they can get more than ever.

In the '50s, the only manufacturing arena was the United States. The only financial market was the United States. When there is a limited supply and an insatiable demand, life is sweet for the lucky few.

Now that's no longer the case. If a company does not focus on the customer, a competitor will—whether that competitor is across the street, across the country, across the ocean, or across the ocean but moving in across the street. More competition triggers more choices for customers, and innovation, speed, service, product variety, and performance must all improve.

Other stakeholders have their own concerns. Investors want a strong bond rating. Stockholders need to agree with key performance measures since their satisfaction impacts everything from top management salaries to corporate takeovers. And employees have to feel critically important to the company's long-term success.

Employees constitute another important stakeholder group. Companies are beginning to realize that the skills, competence, and especially the attitude of their frontline employees—those employees who deal with customers—are critical to the success of the organization. The best product in the world cannot compensate for bad personal service from frontline employees. Therefore, not only are employees important in driving external customer satisfaction, but they are important

It is critical that the employees be included in any process of change.

stakeholders within an organization. It is important to the employees that the company be successful and continue to grow to provide job opportunities. In addition, the employees are a powerful force for changing an organization. Without the involvement of the various employee groups, many companies find change very difficult to achieve. Therefore, it is critical that the employees be included in any process of change.

Another important stakeholder group includes stockholders and investors. These are the owners and lenders of an organization. Their success is obviously dependent upon the success of the organization. The organization fails the stockholders and investors, obviously, by risking their financial investments in the organization. In addition, many investors are selecting organizations whose values are similar to their own. For example, where the organization has operations or investments, whether or not the organization is environmentally active and an environmental leader in the industry, and what type of employment policies the organization follows are all very important considerations to the newly aware stockholder/investor group. Because stockholders and investors are a key source of capital for an organization, it is important that they form part and be considered as part of the organization's strategy.

Organizations often regard the government and other regulators as a necessary evil. However, they have roles in the increasingly sophisticated environment in which organizations currently operate. Therefore, it is imperative that the governmental entities within which an organization operates and the various regulators that oversee the organization be considered during the strategic development process. Organizations that fail to consider government regulators in strategic development often find themselves reacting—as opposed to being proactive— in their dealings with the government agencies.

PRIORITIZING AND EVALUATING STAKEHOLDERS

It is very important to find out the wants and expectations of customers—and all stakeholder groups—by communicating with them. That means listening to and understanding their wants and expectations. Just as importantly, it means communicating what the organization is doing, as a part of its strategy, to satisfy its stakeholders. Research shows that two-thirds of the time customers defect from an organization not because of bad products or services, but because of a failure in communication. The same is undoubtedly true for stakeholder groups.

Communication to stakeholders parallels the customer satisfaction example used earlier— stakeholder satisfaction is also a relationship between perceptions and expectations. To manage stakeholder expectations, top management must begin by defining who they are: external customers, employees (internal customers), stockholders, government agencies, and so forth. Then a strategy or a process has to be developed to systematically understand what those stakeholders want and expect. Depending on the stakeholder, different techniques are used. For customers, companies often use surveys or customer focus groups. For employees, they use surveys, focus groups, or discussions. For stockholders, they use surveys, open meetings, content analysis of the stockholder meetings, or other tools to identify and understand wants over a period of time.

Once stakeholder wants and expectations have been identified, it is important that the leadership of the organization prioritize them. One tool often used here is the interrelationship digraph (see Chapter 6), which helps companies look at the relationship between different demands and determine which should be met first. Another tool—CoNexus® Software—makes it easier to prioritize stakeholders' needs and wants.

BEST PRACTICES

Companies should look at Best Practices in setting strategy because management needs to know what organizations are capable of doing in their important processes.

Best Practices are, simply, the best ways to perform processes. Companies should look at Best Practices in setting strategy because management needs to know what organizations are capable of doing in their important processes.

There are five primary benefits to this:

- Best Practices break the organization out of its paradigm. Everyone can see that other

CoNexus is a registered trademark of Leadership 2000, Inc.

companies are doing the same things, but in dramatically different ways. Best Practices open the organization up and provide an opportunity to increase creativity—to see things from a different perspective by challenging existing paradigms.

- Best Practices help set targets by letting management observe and understand "quality" in other companies. That allows management to see what is possible and helps them set targets and goals for the organization. Benchmarking internally leads to improvement of 5 to 10 percent; benchmarking externally can lead to a 300 percent improvement.
- Best Practices provide a role model for change. As companies change their processes or their performance measures, it is important that people in the organizations understand what is possible. Best Practices give organizations external role models to help in the change process. Such concrete examples relieve some of the anxiety that companies face when they try new things.
- Best Practices save organizations time, money, and resources by helping them steal good ideas shamelessly, thereby quickening the learning curve.
- Best Practices help companies address leadership problems by shaking up any arrogance or complacency.

People often confuse Best Practices with benchmarking. Benchmarking is a structured method of measuring processes and products against others. It is the metrics of Best Practices; it's an enabler in developing, implementing, and using performance measures. For example, in some hospitals, it can take up to two hours to admit a patient. Many hospitals are benchmarking by looking at hotels for Best Practices in admitting. The benchmark would compare the time it takes hotels to admit a guest—less than one minute—to the time it takes hospitals— more than two hours.

THE ENVIRONMENT

The strategy of an organization is driven by its leadership, the stakeholders, and Best Practices. However, the strategy also is influenced by the environment in which the organization operates, including competition, suppliers and readiness of supply, government regulation, and so forth. It is important that the boundaries between the environment and the strategy be permeable, since business leaders need to scan the environment continually and adjust the strategy as appropriate.

The drivers—leadership, stakeholders, and Best Practices in the environment—are used to develop a strategy that focuses on the vision and mission of the organization. As the strategy is developed and implemented, communication with the stakeholders should continue in order to understand their changing wants and expectations and manage their perceptions. In addition, the strategy of the organization will change as the performance measures are implemented and used. As the company continuously improves its processes and improves its focus on customer and stakeholder wants and expectations, it should likewise change and become more focused.

The strategy of the organization will change as the performance measures are implemented and used.

VITAL SIGNS

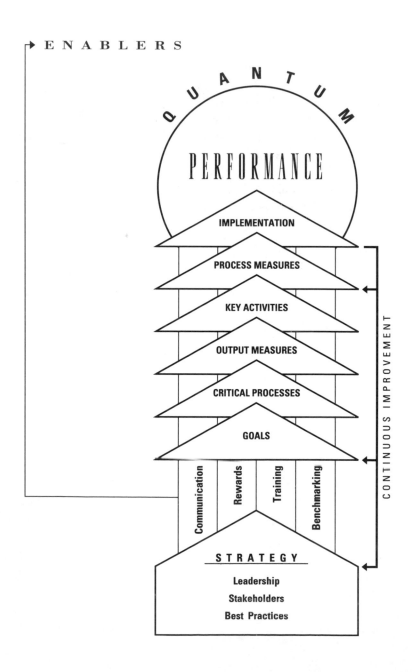

ENABLERS

QUANTUM

PERFORMANCE

IMPLEMENTATION

PROCESS MEASURES

KEY ACTIVITIES

OUTPUT MEASURES

CRITICAL PROCESSES

GOALS

Communication Rewards Training Benchmarking

CONTINUOUS IMPROVEMENT

STRATEGY

Leadership

Stakeholders

Best Practices

ENABLERS

■ **DEFINITION**

The Model defines four enablers—communication, training, rewards, and benchmarking—that help companies develop, implement, and use new performance measures.

● **BENEFITS**

The enablers make it possible for people to change: to "own" the outputs of the model.

▲ **RISKS**

Change causes great stress in organizations; the enablers address the changes required to develop, implement, and use new performance measures and soften their impact.

Everyone agrees: Organizations should have the right performance measures. They should measure people and processes in accordance with the way they want them to perform. In the past few years, new trends have begun to impact performance measurement systems. At the organizational level, for example, is the shift from an inside-out perspective to an outside-in focus on the customer. At the process level is a shift from a functional to a process organizational structure, and at the people level is a shift from individuals to teams.

Yet most companies have still not changed their performance measures over the years, even though there have been many projects or programs initiated to change them.

There's a simple reason for that inertia: The Quantum Performance Measurement Model is easy to talk about, but difficult to implement. It tells a company what to do—the tasks, but management must first get people to "own" the outputs of the Model. We like to refer to this process of ownership as the "enablers" because these help a company successfully develop, implement, and use new performance measures.

A lot of actions may help companies implement performance measures. But the Pareto principle, named after the 19th century economist Vilfredo Pareto (Juran, 1992), suggests that 80 percent of the effects or results come from 20 percent of the possible causes or solutions; 80 percent of the results will come from the use of four key enablers.

The enablers—**communication, training, rewards,** and **benchmarking**—will get organizations 80 percent (or more) of the way through the successful development, implementation, and use of new performance measures. The other 20 percent of actions or tactics will be company-specific, dependent on the individuals involved in the organization and the leadership style.

Each of the four enablers should be used **throughout** the Model; it's too late **after** performance measures are defined and developed.

Why these four enablers? The answer ties back to the concept that performance measurement, in many cases, leads to radical changes in an organization. And of all the possible changes, people perhaps are most sensitive about how they are measured. Change, in and of itself, is often difficult. Changing how people are measured causes great stress on organizations, even if people agree that the current measures are not appropriate and even if people agree that they are not measured properly. Just understanding the new measures and knowing how to work and survive within the system make people resist change. Therefore, the team developing the new performance measurement system must deal with the impact of change throughout the process.

The change process (Figure 4.2) illustrates the impact of change in an organization over time.

The enablers—communication, training, rewards, and benchmarking—will get organizations 80 percent (or more) of the way through the successful development, implementation, and use of new performance measures.

Changing how people are measured causes great stress on organizations.

FIGURE 4.2
THE CHANGE PROCESS

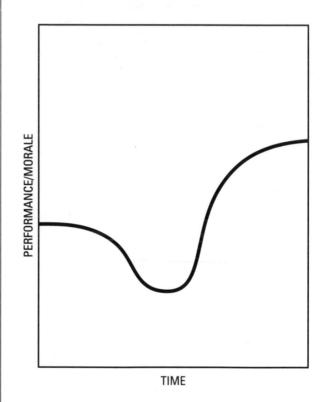

The X axis is time; the Y axis is performance or
the morale of people in an organization. Before
a change is announced, an organization's
performance or employee morale is at the status quo
level. After the change is announced, performance
or morale typically declines for a while.

When I was explaining the change process to
a group at one of my clients, the president of
the company started laughing. That would have
been okay if I had been trying to be funny. But
I wasn't. As I continued discussing the change
process, the president continued laughing. In
fact, after a few minutes, he had tears rolling
down his face. It's intimidating to stand in
front of a client, especially the president and his
direct reports, and have a serious, thoughtful
discussion on change while the president is
laughing hysterically. So I stopped and asked
him why he was laughing. He told this story.

That morning, he had had a breakfast meeting
with his eight regional sales managers to
announce a new sales commission policy: The
company was to increase both the commission
rates and the product lines and, instead of being
paid commissions after two weeks, the sales
force would get the commissions after one
week. In summary, the news was only good:
more money, faster, for more products.

See Scott & Jaffe (1988), Pascarella (1987), and Beer, Eisenstat
and Spector (1990) listed under References for additional
discussions on the impact of change in organizations.

By 11:00 a.m., the president had fielded approximately 75 phone calls from the sales force asking why he was changing the sales strategy. So even though this change was beneficial to the sales force, no one sold any product that day. The reason: The sales force was not involved in the decision. The announcement was the first time they had heard about the change, and they were caught off guard.

Since the results illustrated by the change process are predictable, it is important to **manage its intensity** or the extent of the decline and the **time or duration** of the process.

To minimize the intensity and duration of the change process during [the] implementation [of performance measures], enablers are used.

To minimize the intensity and duration of the change process during and throughout the implementation of the Quantum Performance Measurement Model, the enablers are used.

Communication as well as training are used to manage the intensity; rewards and benchmarking are used to manage the duration of the process (Figure 4.3).

COMMUNICATION

Companies manage the intensity of the change process by developing and implementing a two-way communication strategy. The reason the president's sales force had such a severe reaction to the changes in the sales commissions, product line, and payment schedule was not because the changes were good or bad. It was because

FIGURE 4.3
MANAGING THE CHANGE PROCESS

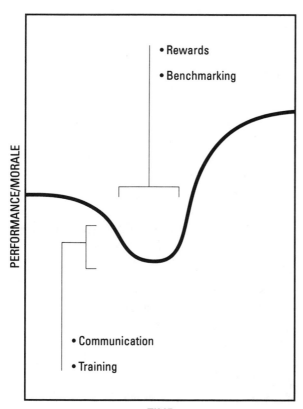

they were a surprise. No one had told the salespeople that changes were being contemplated. No one had asked their opinion or listened to their ideas in the design of the new commission policies.

Communication is an exchange of ideas.

Many companies understand—sort of—the importance of communicating with their employees; however, they feel that this can be done through posting signs on bulletin boards, by putting articles in the company newspaper, or by starting newsletters to cover certain projects and initiatives. These are all legitimate ways of getting messages out, but they're not necessarily communication. The definition of communication that works in the Model is an **exchange of ideas,** and that word **exchange** is very important.

What is needed is more than the broadcasting of messages to employees; what's also required is listening to employees voice concerns, ideas, and input in formal and informal ways throughout the implementation of the Quantum Performance Measurement Model. This exchange of ideas often must take place on a very personal level—one on one and in small groups—as opposed to traditional broadcasting methods.

A communication strategy should be developed at the beginning of the Quantum Performance Measurement Model. Since communication is an enabler, the strategy has to consider that the time frame is the duration of the development process. The strategy should also take into account that communication must be not only vertical (from the top down) but also horizontal.

Many times organizations use a communication strategy that mirrors their traditional financial budgetary process. That is, people in charge of the budget within "functional silos" communicate only with those who report to them, and so forth, down throughout the organization. That is fine, but it includes only one of the organization's dimensions.

A horizontal communication strategy shares the same characteristics as cross-functional processes. In addition, it facilitates a bottom-up exchange of ideas.

A good communication strategy assesses **formal** channels (bulletin boards, articles in the company press, newsletters) as well as **informal** channels. Management knows *who* is listened to in an organization—the individuals and groups whom the employees respect. These people must be a part of the communication strategy because employees often trust these informal channels more than the formal ones.

The issue here is perhaps best described by Gloria J. Gery in her book, *Electronic Performance Support Systems (1991)*: "Most people are afraid to listen, because what they hear will make them change." Since communication, as defined and used in the Model, represents an exchange of ideas, the Model should be used to make changes in the processes people perform. The employees of an organization must feel that their voices are being heard.

A technique that is often used to facilitate effective two-way communication in organizations is structured brainstorming, which provides an opportunity for employees to voice ideas and concerns in a nonjudgmental atmosphere. Too often, new ideas are generated and evaluated in the same meeting. This discourages honest dialogue and creativity. Structured brainstorming is characterized by a focus on specific topics, a framework that encourages participation from all members, and a process that separates the idea giver from the idea.

TRAINING

Training itself is a process— not an event.

The second enabler used to manage the intensity or the extent of decline in the change process is training. In the Model, training helps to impart management skills. It is important for management to recognize that training itself is a process— not an event. Training should be continuous throughout the entire Model; training is a process **within** the Model.

As part of the Quantum Performance Measurement Model, people receive the appropriate training. They are given the opportunity to learn the critical skills needed to develop, implement, and use performance measures: interpersonal skills (listening, effective meeting, facilitation, presentation, team building), process mapping, statistics and fact gathering, problem solving, and even planning.

Management skills training is essential in the process. Middle management often resists new performance measures because the measures initiate employee empowerment, which, in turn, can "disempower" management. To avoid this resistance, these managers need to be trained in skills that will support their new role.

One of the reasons the change process occurs—or one of the reasons why people don't like change—is that people are comfortable in what they do because they know how to do it. Better the devil they know than the devil they don't. And since they find comfort in the status quo, their performance or morale declines when change is introduced. Training helps alleviate this anxiety by providing people with the skills and knowledge they need in the new environment. In addition, the Quantum Performance Measurement Model itself requires skills in the design, implementation, and monitoring of new performance measures. Training is a critical part of acquiring these skills.

Training helps alleviate this anxiety by providing people with the skills and knowledge they need in the new environment.

Training must be specific to the people in the organization. Today, many companies are looking at training as the Holy Grail in their quest for improved performance. In the '70s, the Holy Grail was MRPII systems in manufacturing. In the '80s, it was computer-integrated manufacturing. In the early '90s, it seems to be training. Companies believe that if they send all their people away for training for two or three weeks, they'll come back and

Training must be specific to the people in the organization.

beat the socks off the competition. Nothing can
be further from the truth. In fact, what happens
in many cases is that, although the training
itself may be very good, people go back to
an environment with the old performance
measurement system, the old leadership and
management style, the old processes, and the lack
of authority, the lack of communication systems,
rewards, and benchmarking. Nothing changes.

What is important is that training enables change
to take place. In the Training diagram (Figure
4.4), the C curve represents traditional training.
People go to seminars; whether good or bad, it
doesn't really matter. During the training event,
their awareness of the problems is increased,
but immediately after the seminar they forget.
Consequently, the expected improvement
in performance does not occur.

The B curve occurs when companies augment
lectures with case studies and practice sessions.
Again, the training is probably pretty good.
Participants receive good information, and
they have the opportunity to apply their new
knowledge. After the training event, performance
increases slightly because participants had the
opportunity to practice new skills. But the
employees do not achieve the required
performance level because they have to apply
new skills in the old system with its wrong
performance measures, undefined processes,
and lack of support.

FIGURE 4.4
TRAINING
Adapted from Gery (1991). Used with the permission of
Gloria J. Gery and Weingarten Publications, Inc.

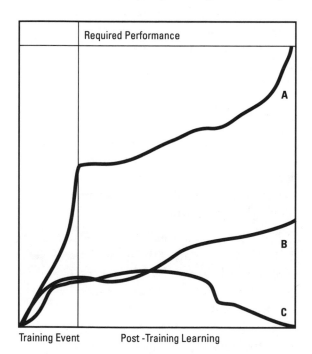

TIME AND EXPERIENCE

The third curve—the A curve—represents training within the Model. While it also includes lecture and practice or case studies, support **after** the training enables people to use their new skills while being supervised by those within the organization who know the subject matter. In other words, employees are "mentored" and supported after the formal training event.

The A curve is JIT training; that is, training delivered just-in-time, right before it's needed. During the training event itself, people become aware of concepts they'll use that day, or the next day, on the job. Then, after the training event, individuals move from concept buy-in to ownership.

Just as communication and training are used to deal with the intensity of the change process, we also have enablers to reduce the time (duration) of the change process. These enablers are **rewards** and **benchmarking.**

REWARDS

A reward system allow[s] the company to motivate people… to "stay the course" of change.

One of the problems with change, and one of the key issues in the Model, is getting people to "stay the course." It is very easy to be enthusiastic at the beginning of a project. But performance measurement is not a project; it is a process. It is a very long, very difficult process that impacts an entire organization, from strategy to people on the line. As the performance or morale of these people declines, it's difficult for them to see that there is an up slope—that things will get better. In the midst of the change, they see nothing but more decline. It is important, then, that a reward system allow the company to motivate people during the implementation of the Model to "stay the course" of change. What is important to remember here is that rewards need to be meaningful to the parties impacted: Employees are the "customers" of the reward system.

Rewards need to be meaningful to the parties impacted.

The definition we use for "rewards" is something given in return for service or accomplishment. This is not necessarily money, although there seems to be a disturbing trend in many companies for management to believe that money is the only way to reward people. The problem with monetary awards is that they typically make "winners" and "losers" out of the employees: those who get money versus those who don't. This creates nothing but divisiveness and does not help in achieving change, since change has to take place cross-functionally through a team approach. Selecting individuals for monetary rewards does not help the team concept.

"Rewards" [are] something given in return for service or accomplishment...not necessarily money.

Since the performance measures developed in the Model show how to act to meet company goals, they must also link directly to the performance appraisal system. In other words, people must be evaluated by the same measures used for their work.

Examples of rewards that companies use successfully include new responsibilities and promotions, time off with pay, and public recognition in local newspapers or just among their associates. A letter from top management to an employee can be a powerful reward. And when the letter is sent home, the employee's family can share in the recognition. The key is to have an approach that includes many different rewards.

BENCHMARKING

The fourth enabler in the Quantum Performance Measurement Model is benchmarking (see Chapter 3). Recall that Best Practices are, simply, the best ways to do a process and that benchmarking is integral to Best Practices because it provides the metrics used in Best Practices. As the standard of comparison, benchmarking is very important in the change process.

Benchmarking allows companies to measure from their "as is" position to their "should be" position.

As companies enter the change process, they have to see across to the other side. Other people and organizations have succeeded where they are now venturing. Benchmarking allows companies to see that, since others have accomplished these goals, they too can accomplish them. It shows companies where they should be. It allows companies to measure from their "as is" position to their "should be" position.

The benefits of benchmarking are great. First, benchmarking provides directions for meeting and exceeding customer wants. It shows companies what can be done. And, like Best Practices, benchmarking does not have to be industry-specific. Organizations in one industry can benchmark against organizations in different industries to find out how they can meet and exceed their customers' wants.

Second, benchmarking helps establish customer-focused goals. If one organization has obtained customer response time of less than five minutes, then maybe that's the appropriate performance target. Benchmarking allows companies to move from simple, continuous, incremental improvement to thinking that is "out of the ordinary"—extraordinary.

Third, benchmarking raises awareness of Best Practices. By making benchmarking part of the continuous model of designing, implementing, and using performance measures, companies make possible the achievement of Quantum Performance.

One of the key failures of many performance measurement projects is that companies ignore the enablers until it is too late. Companies know that communication is important, but they view it as a broadcast of corporate messages, rather than an exchange of ideas. Companies know that training is important, but they don't do training until the end. Companies know that rewards are important, yet their appraisal systems are not linked to the performance measures. And

One of the key failures of many performance measurement projects is that companies ignore the enablers until it is too late.

companies know there is a lot to learn from others, yet they do not benchmark against other organizations.

The enablers must be used throughout the Model, beginning with the development of the strategy. The Quantum Performance Measurement Model shows how the enablers are integrated into, and are driven from, the strategy of the organization. Therefore, the enablers must be instituted early and used continuously throughout the Model— throughout the design, implementation, and use of performance measurement activities.

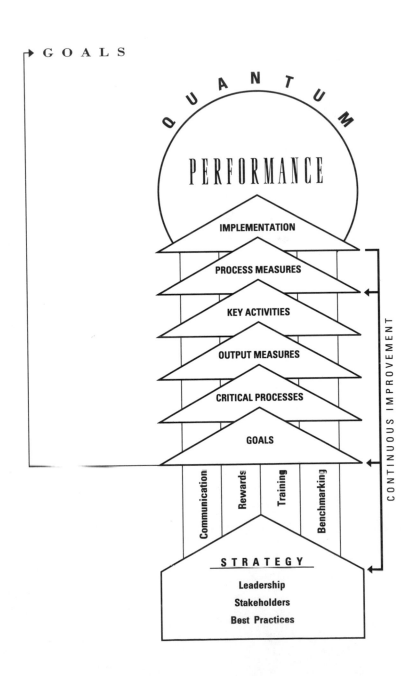

VITAL SIGNS

GOALS

QUANTUM

PERFORMANCE

IMPLEMENTATION

PROCESS MEASURES

KEY ACTIVITIES

OUTPUT MEASURES

CRITICAL PROCESSES

GOALS

Communication

Rewards

Training

Benchmarking

CONTINUOUS IMPROVEMENT

STRATEGY

Leadership

Stakeholders

Best Practices

5

GOALS

■ **DEFINITION**
Goals are the performance results desired in the future;
they "operationalize" the company's strategy.

● **BENEFITS**
Quantum Performance requires management to set
goals for cost, quality, and time that move beyond
competitive advantage to establish new boundaries
of performance.

▲ **RISKS**
Management must be careful not to focus exclusively
on conventional financial measures since these do
not support continuous improvement.

Goals are the performance results desired in the future.

Organizations need to operationalize their strategy by setting goals, which are the performance results desired in the future.

Goals should be developed iteratively by management and the people responsible for processes, who must buy in and concur with goals in order to reach them. The goals need to cascade down through the organization, with management at each level taking responsibility for the goal-setting process.

The overall goal for a company today is **Quantum Performance.** Goal setting for cost, quality, and time begins with **benchmarking**—to discover industry and process-specific Best Practices—and then moves **beyond competitive advantage** to establish new boundaries of performance.

BENCHMARKING

Benchmarking focuses on the performance and operations issues— cost, quality, and time—that drive a competitive difference.

Benchmarking (see Chapter 4) helps companies set goals for process improvement by asking the key question: How well are we performing relative to the competition? Benchmarking can be by product—"Here's how our product performs. Here's what our customers think about it." Or it can be by process—"How many employees do we have? What's our capacity? How much does it cost us to provide a service?" Benchmarking focuses on the performance and operations issues—cost, quality, and time—that drive a competitive difference.

When choosing competitors to include in a benchmarking analysis, it is important to select

two different types: (1) tried-and-true
competitors with equal or greater strength,
market share, global reach, and products; and
(2) up-and-coming companies that have, as
yet, no significant market share but are likely
to have innovative technologies, materials,
designs, and flexible organizational structures.

The objective of benchmarking is to measure
Best Practices in terms of price, quality, delivery,
service, technology, and product performance.
The theory behind this is simple: Given a
choice, a consumer will choose the best product
value with the best service.

There are three types of benchmarking: internal,
competitive, and world-class.

Internal benchmarking: A company analyzes
and compares similar processes within its own
organization. For example, a company with
multiple locations might benchmark the various
personnel departments. Manufacturers with
multiple plants could benchmark processes or
even equipment. A single plant with duplicated
equipment could benchmark activities such
as setup time. Why would a 400-ton press in
one part of the plant require 30 minutes to set
up, while the same 400-ton press in another
area requires only 7 minutes? With internal
benchmarking, opportunities for improvement
are clear.

Competitive benchmarking: A company
compares its processes or outputs of processes

against those of its competitors. Competitive benchmarking can be very difficult because of the understandable reluctance of competing companies to share confidential information or to show similar processes. For this reason, competitive benchmarking is often done on the macro level through industry statistics and averages. However, too many variables can distort macro benchmarks and limit their relevance. Take, for example, how banks compare themselves against one another for loan loss reserves. Given such factors as size and type of market, what do such indices reveal? Not much, really. All a bank's management can say with certainty is that the institution stands in a specific quartile within a given population. To understand what really matters, one must know the processes.

When performing competitive benchmarking, remember **customers.** The "best performance" in the world can be just wasted energy if there's no customer need, want, or expectation.

Example: The management of General Motors was particularly proud of the company's car window defroster. The most powerful made, it did the job in 15 seconds. The problem? Customers didn't care. The significantly cheaper—and quieter— version in Japanese cars took two minutes. For customers, time was not important; price (cost) and noise (quality) were.

World-class benchmarking: A company compares a function or process in its organization to the same or similar function or process in a "best of the best" company, regardless of industry. In other words, to look at the best distribution function, a manufacturer might visit a wholesaler/distributor's operations. Perhaps a hotel has the best customer check-in process and can serve as a model for a hospital. When a world-class or "best of the best" company does not compete with the inquiring company, it's often willing to share information and allow access to its operations and processes.

TARGET COSTING

A relatively new benchmarking technique—target costing—addresses product cost over the entire product life cycle. It is used for both strategic analysis and operational control. The process of target costing gives information to management on the goals that need to be set for cost, quality, and time. The term "target cost" is probably inaccurate. "Target performance measure" is better. Once performance is focused, once performance is **targeted,** costs will follow. Only an understanding of customers and processes allows management to target performance.

For a given product, the target cost is the maximum manufactured cost that will allow an expected return while enabling a company to gain share within a market niche. Close behind the first question, "What do customers want?" is a second: "How can the product be made at a cost that provides a sufficient return?" This is the question that target costing tries to answer.

Target costing gives information to management on the goals that need to be set for cost, quality, and time.

Target costing has been used successfully by companies and industries noted for short product life cycles in rapidly changing markets.

Example: Automotive and electronics companies saw target costing as a way to define a future cost for a new product that had to hit the ground running—one that had to satisfy customer expectations and requirements in terms of cost, quality, performance, and service attributes— if it hoped to garner any market share.

For such products, from cars to VCRs, working down an "experience curve" and squeezing out costs "after the fact" were luxuries no longer allowed by the consumer or by the competition. Because these markets are so competitive, consumers will not pay for products that cost more than anticipated or for designs that do not meet their needs or include features that they don't necessarily want.

"Targets" for the design and production of a product and all its components reflect both customer demands and competitors' performance.

The theory behind target costing is this: During the design and development stage, a manufacturer sets "targets" for the design and production of a product and all its components. These targets reflect both customer demands and competitors' performance. If the targets are met, a new product can actually be cost-competitive early in its life cycle and gain the planned level of market share.

In the past few years, this view of target costing has been expanded. Not only is target costing a way to determine and manage a product in development, it's also a technique for **continuous**

improvement. Target costing gives management a new look at old products and provides a way to revitalize them.

What's the connection between target costing and conventional cost accounting? Cost accounting systems are passive and historical. They **identify** and **solve** problems by measuring variances in labor efficiency and rate, material price and usage, fixed and variable overhead spending, efficiency, and inventory value. The problem is that consumption cost information does not deal with quality performance or time performance.

Consumption cost information does not deal with quality performance or time performance.

Target costing, on the other hand, identifies ways to reduce overall product cost, support a faster product development cycle, and diminish the risk of new product introductions. It helps set quality, cost, and time goals in an organization. Target costs identify cost drivers, such as product complexity, before the product is produced so that action, such as simplifying the design, can be taken before actual production begins.

An example of target costing is what Toyota achieved with the Lexus car (Van Hull, 1992). Toyota "targeted" Mercedes car buyers in the United States. Toyota identified its target customers' wants and expectations, including how much they were willing to pay for a certain level of quality, the value they expected. This company understands processes and its target customers very well.

From the two, it set a target cost for the product in order to generate a target profit with a target price:

Target Cost = Target Price – Target Profit

It is important to recognize that just as our definition of the cost category in the Matrix is the economics of "goodness," target cost includes the cost, the revenues (price), and the profits. It is the economics of the product. Toyota focused its efforts (set its goals) by setting performance measures from a cost, quality, and time perspective to achieve a given share strategy.

Target costing is, first and foremost, customer-driven. It begins with an **external** look at what the market demands and how competitors and the best company performing a process meets these demands—for price, performance, quality, reliability, durability, delivery, and service—through product design, process design, and management of the cost structure.

The intent of target costing is to reduce total product cost (over the entire life cycle) by minimizing the costs of investment, product design, production, and distribution.

The intent of target costing is to reduce **total** product cost (over the entire life cycle) by minimizing the costs of investment, product design, production, and distribution. Target costing is an up-front planning technique with strategic significance, not an after-the-fact record-keeping system. It requires an understanding of the market values and trends, competitors, and—most of all—one's own processes.

CONTINUOUS IMPROVEMENT

The purpose of target costing is not day-to-day cost control. Instead, target costing affects product competitiveness by influencing design specifications (quality) and production techniques (time). Since as much as 80 percent of a product's costs are determined during the design stage, target costing attempts to ensure that, from the beginning, products that meet and exceed customer needs are made at an optimum cost and in a reduced lead time.

Target costing promotes continuous improvement through the elimination of waste activities over the entire design and production cycle. Target costs are "ideals"; they are generally developed by taking the best product designs in the industry and combining them with the most cost-effective manufacturing operations.

How does an organization define and achieve a target? That can be a complex challenge, since to be effective, target costing has to be applied to more than the final product (whose likely market price points and subsequent target cost might be relatively easy to "guesstimate").

While there's no single methodology or cast-in-stone steps to follow, a target costing process generally includes four efforts:

First, **internal analysis:** A company must understand its own processes in order to find the activities and cost drivers within product designs and production processes and to eliminate

Target costing promotes continuous improvement through the elimination of waste activities over the entire design and production cycle.

nonvalue-added activities. In other words, **process mapping** and **activity-based costing** (see Chapter 8), when part of target costing, lead to the development of production processes that are both efficient and effective.

Second, **external analysis:** An organization must understand the external environment, including customer requirements and competitors' products/processes. Here are just two tools that can be used:

Market research: Target cost is affected by different customer demands and expectations: price, quality, delivery, service, technology, and product performance. Market research weighs the value of each of these factors, as well as their relative importance and interaction. What's important here is that management use market information to improve **processes** as well as products. Market research is not new. It has traditionally been used to make a company's advertising or marketing campaign more effective. The problem is that market research has not been used to design, develop, produce, or deliver the product or service.

Quality Functional Deployment (QFD) is a technique that translates the characteristics important to customers into product design parameters (Akao, 1988). These are then compared to the market's assessment of competitors' products. Together, market research and QFD answer a key question posed by target costing: What product features does (will) the market value? With this information in hand, the manufacturer can work backwards. Customers' needs, wants, and expectations are used to define the cost/performance parameters for new products **before** and **while** they are in the conceptual design and development stage.

Third, **product/process design:** Two concepts, value engineering and supplier involvement, are critical here.

Value engineering: The first two steps in target costing provide the information needed to "build in" quality. Value engineering (Reddy, 1991) asks: "How do we improve our product/process designs to meet the 'ideal' time performance measures?" (Note: The targets must be realistic, or they won't be credible. On the other hand, the targets have to force the company to "reach" a bit or they won't trigger continuous improvement.)

Value engineering means testing "what if" scenarios based on differences in materials, design parameters, and production processes. Over the product's life cycle, targets can be used to establish continuous improvement. At the start of production, for example, the target cost is refined to reflect both lessons learned during production trials and expected improvements down the learning curve.

Supplier involvement: If suppliers do not provide input on ways to meet target cost, quality, and time goals, the manufacturer may, by default, make suboptimal decisions about material selection, assembly techniques, and product/process design.

Suppliers should be part of the whole target-costing process.

Dictating targets to the supplier is not sufficient, productive, or appropriate. Rather, suppliers should be part of the whole target-costing process. By sharing information, both manufacturer and supplier can understand customer requirements, competitor performance, and their own processes.

Fourth, **performance measurement:** Using the Matrix and Model, new performance measures can be defined to support continuous improvement.

Target costing helps a company know its competitive position vis-á-vis costs within its industry; identify the relevant, and often hidden, costs of products; isolate areas of high costs for each product and compare these to the competition or Best Practices; and set targets and find ways to reduce costs to meet goals.

Target costing is not without pitfalls.

But target costing is not without pitfalls.

First, a lot of companies try to compare their performance to the competition's or Best Practices yet do **not** understand their own processes. (Steps 1 and 2 are often performed simultaneously, but Step 2 should not be performed **without** Step 1.)

Second, many companies try to do too much, too fast. They try to "target cost" the entire company, and they get lost in the mass of detail. What is important? First, companies need a systematic approach to understanding processes.

Then these processes must be compared to the practices of the competition.

Third, management has to restructure the company's internal performance management system. In other words, a new model should reflect the results of target-costing analyses and focus on processes and activities.

The first step of the Quantum Performance Measurement Model is setting goals. These goals should be driven by the company's strategy and based in facts, not simply management's opinion. The facts can come from many sources, including benchmarking and target costing activities.

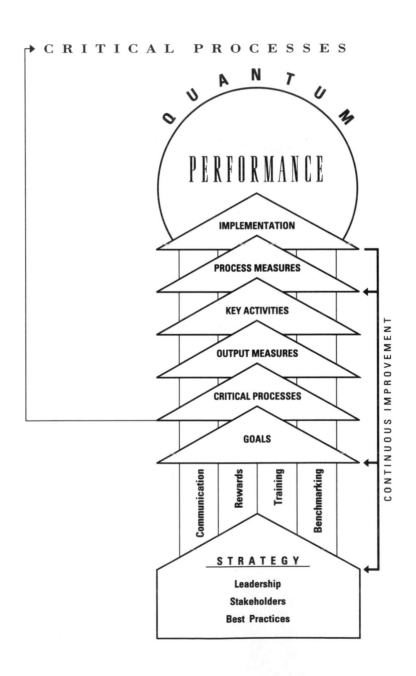

VITAL SIGNS

CRITICAL PROCESSES

QUANTUM

PERFORMANCE

IMPLEMENTATION

PROCESS MEASURES

KEY ACTIVITIES

OUTPUT MEASURES

CRITICAL PROCESSES

GOALS

Communication Rewards Training Benchmarking

STRATEGY

Leadership
Stakeholders
Best Practices

CONTINUOUS IMPROVEMENT

6

CRITICAL
PROCESSES

■ **DEFINITION**

A process is a series of activities that consume resources and produce a product or service.

● **BENEFITS**

By identifying and focusing on critical processes, management improves those areas that are necessary to the survival of the organization.

▲ **RISKS**

Processes are cross-functional. If management focuses on functional performance, overall results will be suboptimal. If goals and performance measures are developed independently, each function will improve only at the expense of others.

As discussed in Chapter 1, a process is a series of activities that consume resources and produce a product or service. Most organizations are organized and managed functionally—such as marketing, sales, manufacturing, research and development, and finance.

Geary Rummler and Alan Brache, in their book *Improving Performance: Managing the White Space on the Organization Chart* (1990), state that the traditional organization chart that most people draw when asked to depict their company or department shows only the vertical reporting relations of the various functions in the organization. This kind of chart is shown in Figure 6.2.

To truly understand and improve an organization, one must focus on its processes

Yet, organizations serve customers through processes that cut **across** functions. If management focuses only on functional performance, overall results will be suboptimal because each function develops goals and performance measures independently and can improve only at the expense of others. Therefore, to truly understand and improve an organization, one must focus on its **processes.**

The process of developing performance measures is a cascading one, starting with the strategy of the organization or unit, and rolling down to goal setting and the identification of critical processes. These processes are required to achieve the goals and, therefore, the strategy.

It is important to identify critical processes because this filtering process keeps everyone focused on

FIGURE 6.2
**FUNCTIONAL
ORGANIZATION CHART**

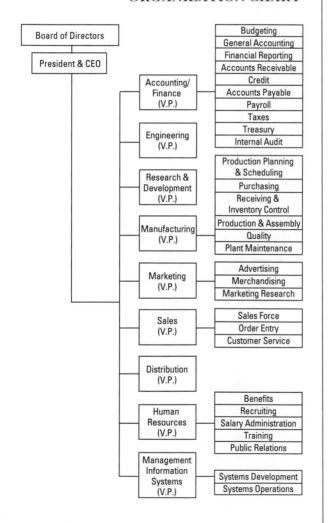

FIGURE 6.3
TYPES OF PROCESSES
Adapted from Rummler (1992).
Used with the permission of The Rummler-Brache Group.

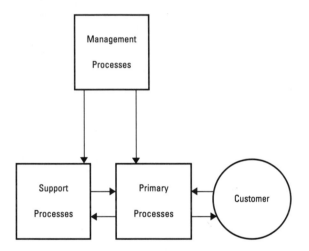

what's truly important to the organization. It also helps management develop, install, and use performance measures first in those areas that are critical to the survival of the organization.

The real questions are: Which are the critical processes? And how does one prioritize them? First, it's necessary to know how to identify processes—critical or not. To do this, one always starts with the customer. Too often, people within a company talk among themselves about what they do; with this internal orientation, they usually end up examining functions, not processes. But starting with the customer—and viewing an organization through the eyes of the customer— gives people an understanding of processes that serve the customer.

Starting with the customer—and viewing an organization through the eyes of the customer—gives people an understanding of processes that serve the customer.

Rummler (1992) proposes three types of processes, as shown in Figure 6.3.

Primary processes are those that touch the customer. If there is a failure in a primary process, the customer will immediately know. These processes include such things as product/service delivery, new product/service development, and production. When one identifies processes, starting with the customer, the primary processes appear first. By looking at processes that touch the customer, a company can often use a simple process to a competitive advantage. For example, MCI can offer its

FIGURE 6.4
GENERIC PROCESSES
Reprinted from Rummler (1992).
Used with the permission of The Rummler-Brache Group.

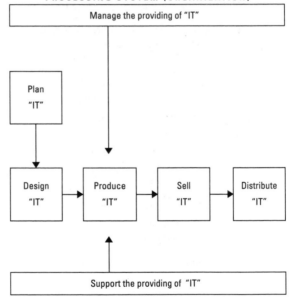

PROCESSING SYSTEM (ORGANIZATION)

"Friends and Neighbors" service line because of the flexibility of its billing process, often viewed as a routine and unimportant process. However, since bills go directly to the customers, the billing process is a primary process.

Support processes support primary ones and are required to perform the primary processes. If there is a failure in a support process, customers will not see that failure immediately. However, the failure eventually will become obvious because it will cause the primary processes to deteriorate. Examples of support processes include processes for human resource management, capital budgeting, and cash and fixed-asset management. Manufacturing would include manufacturing resources planning (MRP) as a support process.

Management processes are required to coordinate the activities of support and primary processes. Examples of this third type of process include quality processes, strategic planning, and management information.

There are some processes common to all companies (see Figure 6.4). All companies provide "something." To do so, they plan, design, produce, sell, and distribute "something." These generic processes can be identified in more detail by industry. In manufacturing, for example, there are several processes that can be grouped by how they interface with the market and suppliers, the environment, and the competition (Figure 6.5).

FIGURE 6.5
MANUFACTURING
PROCESSING SYSTEM
Adapted from Rummler and Brache (1990).
Used with the permission of Jossey-Bass, Inc.

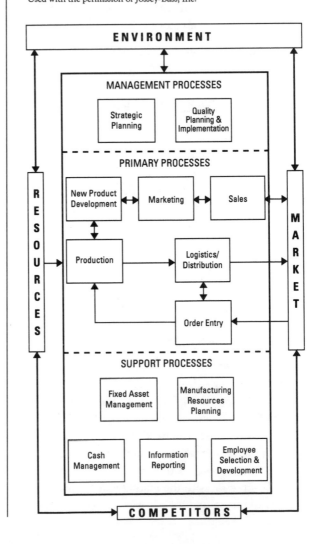

It's important to understand whether a specific process is primary, support, or management because this influences the types of goals that are set. If a company faces global competition, then primary processes (ones that touch the customer) must be world-class. Goals should be developed by looking at world-class companies that perform the same processes, even if they are not within the same industry. At the same time, while support processes must be efficient and effective, they need not necessarily be world-class. And finally, management processes should be minimized. An organization should benchmark to set goals for management processes to be limited and unobtrusive.

After the processes of an organization are identified, they are sorted into primary, support, and management categories to enable prioritization and goal setting to support the organization's strategies. Then the critical processes that directly impact the achievement of the strategies and goals—a combination of primary, support, and management processes—have to be selected. These critical processes require the performance measures to achieve the simultaneous goals of cost, quality, and time, especially in the eyes of the customer.

This work is done by the Performance Measurement Team (see Chapter 10), using the management and planning tools traditionally used to identify qualitative information in organizations.

It's important to understand whether a specific process is primary, support, or management because this influences the types of goals that are set.

Critical processes [are those that] directly impact the achievement of the strategies and goals.

The following definitions of management and planning tools are adapted from **The Memory Jogger Plus+**™ (1989) by Michael Brassard, which should be referred to for details on how to use these tools. The descriptions of the uses of these tools in the area of performance measurement are mine.

Affinity Diagram: This tool (Figure 6.6) is used to gather large amounts of language, that is, qualitative data (ideas, opinions, issues, etc.) and organize it into groupings based on the natural relationships among the items. It is largely a creative rather than a logical process.

An affinity diagram is **not** suggested for use when a problem is simple or requires a very quick solution. The affinity diagram is most helpful when facts or thoughts are in chaos, issues are too large or complex to grasp, a breakthrough in traditional concepts is needed, and support for a solution is essential for successful implementation.

The Performance Measurement Team can use the affinity diagram to brainstorm the company's processes and organize them. After a brief discussion to identify processes and their importance, the Performance Measurement Team writes all of these processes on a 3x5 removable adhesive-backed note.

FIGURE 6.6
AFFINITY
DIAGRAM

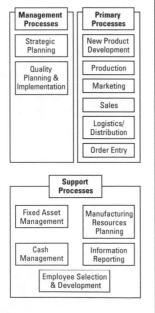

The seven management and planning tools adapted with permission from *The Memory Jogger Plus+: Featuring the Seven Management and Planning Tools*. pp. 17-19, 41-42, 73, 75, 99-101, 135-136, 171-173, 201, 214, by Michael Brassard. Copyright ©1989 GOAL/QPC, 13 Branch Street, Methuen, MA 01844-1953. Tel: 508-685-3900.

Next, the Performance Measurement Team posts the processes on the wall and groups them into associated categories. On another removable adhesive-backed note, the team agrees upon a name for all the processes in that category and the customer for each major category of processes.

After the major headings (processes) are identified, the Performance Measurement Team finally groups the processes into the primary, support, and management categories discussed earlier in this chapter.

Interrelationship Digraph (I.D.): This tool (Figure 6.7) takes complex problems with multiple variables or desired outcomes and explores and displays all of the interrelated factors involved. It graphically shows the logical (and often causal) relationships between factors.

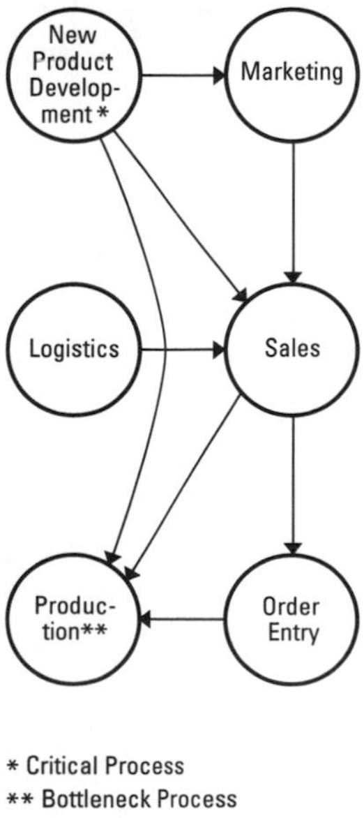

If the Performance Measurement Team has had problems identifying the organization's critical processes, it can use an interrelationship digraph. After identifying the processes on removable adhesive-backed notes, the team posts the notes on a flipchart. Looking at each process, the team addresses this question: "What other process has a major impact on performing the process in question?" A line with an arrow is drawn from that process to the process under investigation.

The next question that the team answers is: "What other processes does this process impact?" Then a line with an arrow is drawn from the

FIGURE 6.7
**INTER-
RELATIONSHIP
DIGRAPH**

* Critical Process
** Bottleneck Process

117

process under investigation to the ones that
are impacted.

After drawing all the lines, the team counts the
lines coming into and going out of each process.
If the process with the **most** outgoing arrows is
improved, this will have a spillover effect on a
large number of other processes. The process with
a large number of arrows coming into it may
be a bottleneck and may need to be fixed before
other processes can be improved.

FIGURE 6.8
TREE DIAGRAM

Tree Diagram: This tool systematically maps out,
in increasing detail, the full range of paths and
tasks that need to be accomplished to achieve a
primary goal and its related subgoals. Graphically,
a tree diagram resembles an organization chart
or family tree. This tool should be used when
a specific task has become the focus but is
not a simple "assignable job," it is known
(or suspected) that implementation will be
complex, there are strong consequences for
missing key tasks (e.g., safety or legal compliance
issues), or a task has run into repeated roadblocks
in implementation.

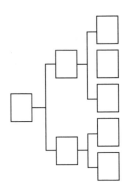

The Performance Measurement Team can use the
tree diagram to plan the tasks necessary to design
and implement new performance measures.

Tree diagram adapted with permission from *The Memory Jogger
Plus+: Featuring the Seven Management and Planning Tools.*
p. 5, by Michael Brassard. Copyright ©1989 GOAL/QPC, 13
Branch Street, Methuen, MA 01844-1953. Tel: 508-685-3900.

Prioritization Matrices: These tools take tasks, issues, or possible actions and prioritize them based on known, weighted criteria. They utilize a combination of the previously mentioned tree diagram and matrix diagram (discussed later in this chapter) techniques, thus narrowing down options to those that are the most desirable or effective. Figure 6.9 provides an example of a prioritization matrix.

The traditional "shoot from the hip" planning process has the apparent advantage of creating fewer options, but it is often the result of conventional thinking. Prioritization matrices are designed to rationally narrow the focus before detailed implementation planning can happen.

Prioritization matrices should be used when the key issues have been identified and the options generated must be narrowed down, the criteria for a "good" solution are agreed upon but there is disagreement over their relative importance, there are limited resources for implementation (e.g., time, funds, human resources), or the options generated have strong interrelationships.

One of the most effective means of gaining group consensus on a company's or department's critical processes is to use the prioritization matrix. To build a prioritization matrix, take the following steps:

- List all processes along the vertical and horizontal sides of the matrix.

FIGURE 6.9
PRIORITIZATION MATRIX
Adapted with permission from *The Memory Jogger Plus+:
Featuring the Seven Management and Planning Tools*. p. 110,
by Michael Brassard. Copyright ©1989. GOAL/QPC,
13 Branch Street, Methuen, MA 01844-1953. Tel: 508-685-3900.

	Employee Selection and Development	Marketing and Selling	Order Fulfillment	New Product Development	Production	Total Across Rows	% of Grand Total	Priority Ranking
Employee Selection and Development		5	.1	.1	.2	5.4	.08	4
Marketing and Selling	.2		.2	.1	.2	.7	.02	5
Order Fulfillment	10	5		.2	.1	15.3	.21	3
New Product Development	10	10	10		.1	30.2	.41	1
Production	5	5	5	5		20	.28	2
Column Total	25.2	25	15.3	7.3	.8	Total Across Columns 73.6 Grand Total		

KEY:
1 Equally Important .1 Less Important
5 More Important .2 Significantly Less Important
10 Significantly More Important

- Compare the importance of each process to every other process using the following scale:

$1 = \dfrac{\text{Equally}}{\text{Important}}$ $.1 = \dfrac{\text{Less}}{\text{Important}}$

$5 = \dfrac{\text{More}}{\text{Important}}$ $.2 = \dfrac{\text{Significantly Less}}{\text{Important}}$

$10 = \dfrac{\text{Significantly}}{\text{More Important}}$

- Add the scores of each column and record the total.
- Add the column totals to reach the grand total.
- Divide each row total by the grand total to convert it to a percentage.
- Rank the processes from the process with the highest percentage to the one with the lowest percentage.

Matrix Diagram: This versatile tool shows the connection (or correlation) between each idea or issue in one group of items and each idea or issue in one or more other groups of items. At each intersecting point between a vertical set of items and horizontal set of items, a relationship is indicated as being either present or absent. In its most common use, the matrix diagram takes the

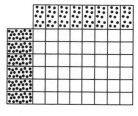

FIGURE 6.10
MATRIX DIAGRAM

Matrix diagram adapted with permission from *The Memory Jogger Plus+: Featuring the Seven Management and Planning Tools.* p. 6, by Michael Brassard. Copyright ©1989 GOAL/QPC, 13 Branch Street, Methuen, MA 01844-1953. Tel: 508-685-3900.

necessary tasks (often from the tree diagram) and graphically displays their relationships with people, functions, or other tasks. This tool is frequently used to determine who has responsibility for the different parts of an implementation plan.

The matrix diagram is used when definable and assignable tasks must be "deployed" to the rest of the organization, the "focused activities" generated must be tested against other things that the organization is already doing, the organization is trying to prioritize present activities given new priorities (i.e., choose the present system(s) that helps achieve the greatest number of new objectives), or there is a need to get a cumulative numerical "score" that allows a comparison of any one item to any other item or to all of the other items combined.

The Performance Measurement Team can use the matrix diagram to identify the critical processes. Along the horizontal side, key customer wants are listed. Along the vertical side of the matrix, the company's or department's processes are listed. Three different symbols indicate a strong, medium, or weak relationship between a customer want and a process. No symbol is used if there is no relationship. The processes with the largest number of symbols indicating a strong relationship are identified as the critical processes.

Process Decision Program Chart (PDPC): This tool (Figure 6.11) maps out every conceivable event and contingency that can occur when moving from a problem statement to the possible solutions. This is used to plan each possible chain of events that needs to happen when the problem or goal is an unfamiliar one.

In the simplest terms possible, a PDPC is used whenever uncertainty exists in a proposed implementation plan. Remember, the task at hand should be one that is either new or unique. A routine task doesn't warrant a PDPC unless a major new factor is introduced, such as a market or personnel change. The implementation plan should have sufficient complexity. If the steps are so few or so clear that deviations are trivial or self-explanatory, then a PDPC would be a wasted effort. The efficiency of the implementation must be critical. If, for instance, there is a 12-month window within which a 3-month plan must be implemented, there is plenty of "slack time" for deviations from the original path.

The Performance Measurement Team can use the process decision program chart, which is actually a tree diagram with contingency steps on the end activities, when developing performance measures and an implementation plan. The team develops a tree diagram and asks: "What if we can't perform this activity?" The countermeasures are then written on the tree diagram under that activity and enclosed in the circle.

Process decision program chart adapted with permission from *The Memory Jogger Plus+: Featuring the Seven Management and Planning Tools*. p. 6, by Michael Brassard. Copyright ©1989 GOAL/QPC, 13 Branch Street, Methuen, MA 01844-1953. Tel: 508-685-3900.

FIGURE 6.11
PROCESS
DECISION
PROGRAM
CHART

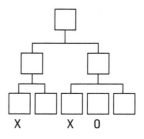

FIGURE 6.12
ACTIVITY
NETWORK
DIAGRAM

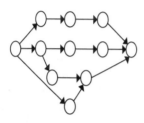

Activity Network Diagram: This tool is used to plan the most appropriate schedule for any complex task and all of its related subtasks. It projects likely completion time and monitors all subtasks for adherence to the necessary schedule. This is used when the task at hand is a familiar one with subtasks that are of a known duration.

The most important criterion (and perhaps the only meaningful one) is that the subtasks, their sequencing, and duration must be well known. If this is not the case, then the construction of the activity network diagram can become a very frustrating experience. When the timing of the actual events is very different from the original diagram, people dismiss the diagram as an exercise that stresses form over substance. When there is a lack of history about an implementation process, the PDPC may provide more insight into a likely implementation schedule. What the PDPC lacks in precise scheduling details is balanced by its realistic picture of the task that must be implemented.

Given these factors, the activity network diagram is most useful when the task is a complex one, the subtasks are familiar ones with known durations, the task at hand is a critical organizational target, there are simultaneous implementation paths

Activity network diagram adapted with permission from *The Memory Jogger Plus+: Featuring the Seven Management and Planning Tools.* p. 6, by Michael Brassard. Copyright ©1989 GOAL/QPC, 13 Branch Street, Methuen, MA 01844-1953. Tel: 508-685-3900.

that must be coordinated, and there is little margin for error in the actual vs. the estimated time to completion.

The seven management and planning tools described in this chapter can help the Performance Measurement Team identify and prioritize the critical processes. The three most useful are the affinity diagram, the interrelationship digraph, and the prioritization matrix.

The seven management and planning tools can help identify and prioritize critical processes.

Once processes have been identified, classified, and prioritized, the Performance Measurement Team begins the process of simplification through process mapping (see Chapter 8). Measures should not be applied to processes that are known to be inefficient, ineffective, excessively complex, redundant, or in any way nonvalue-added. They should be eliminated or simplified first.

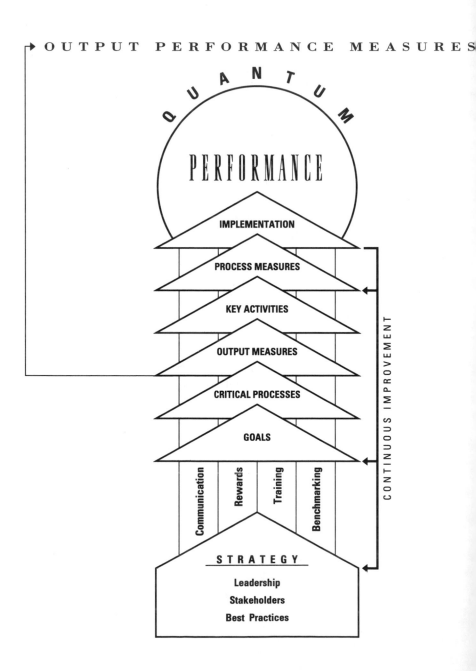

VITAL SIGNS

OUTPUT PERFORMANCE MEASURES

QUANTUM

PERFORMANCE

IMPLEMENTATION

PROCESS MEASURES

KEY ACTIVITIES

OUTPUT MEASURES

CRITICAL PROCESSES

GOALS

Communication Rewards Training Benchmarking

CONTINUOUS IMPROVEMENT

STRATEGY

Leadership

Stakeholders

Best Practices

7

OUTPUT PERFORMANCE MEASURES

■ **DEFINITION**

Output measures report the results of a process and are used to control resources.

● **BENEFITS**

Output measures should include quality and time, as well as cost. New performance standards are emerging for both.

▲ **RISKS**

In most companies, the output performance measures are traditional financial reports. But if these are the **only** measures used, they are insufficient to help management focus on what is important to the customer.

Output performance measures are used to report the results of a process and to control resources and monitor results.

Management is very familiar with output performance measures. These are used to report the results of a process and to control resources and monitor results. In most companies, they are the only kind of performance measures used.

Typically, output performance measures are the traditional financial reports—accounting, the general ledger system, the budget and budgeting system, and the variance system. While these are important, they also are historical and after the fact. Even more important, they address only one member of the family of measures of cost, quality, and time. They aren't "wrong" measures, but they do report to management on only one factor. In the short term, this can encourage a company to optimize cost while suboptimizing quality and time.

Companies must understand their costs and their financial performance. This information needs to be reliable, relevant, and useful because profits keep companies running: They enable companies to hire employees, pay suppliers and vendors, and pay the utility bills. Costs affect decisions about outsourcing, product profitability, product lines, and customer segments.

But for many companies, cost measures are the only ones in place. Why is that a problem? Because traditional cost accounting reports the **results** of a process. As performance measures, costs have all the strengths and weaknesses of output measures in general.

They're directed toward management,
for whom cost is a legitimate concern. But
costs are not always useful or appropriate
at the operational level, where true process
improvement can and should be implemented.
For example, manufacturing is often held
accountable for costs (financial performance),
yet cannot achieve financial objectives
because of problems with the product design
(engineering) or raw materials (procurement).

Output measures are too late. Once costs
are incurred, the problem already has been
going on for a long time. For instance, consider
a company that measures product returns. It
may be interesting to capture that information;
however, the problem—producing a bad
product—has already occurred.

People tend to corrupt processes to achieve
desired results (costs). The process corruption
varies. If the measure is budget variances, for
example, companies may jeopardize their long-
term health by cutting back on necessary R&D
or advertising to achieve a short-term cost goal.
Using a standard cost system as the only measure,
companies let bad product through to achieve
production or cost standards. But then the product
comes back as a product return or warranty cost.
The true cost is customer dissatisfaction.

If budgets are the primary driver, companies ship
half of a quarter's quotas during the final week
of the period to achieve financial results from

quarter to quarter. Again, a higher price is paid in returns and warranties. If a plant manager is evaluated based on labor efficiency, he could achieve labor efficiency by letting a bad product through or by manipulating inventory levels.

Because costs have been around a long time, people know how to manipulate them. But **costs alone do not measure the complexity of today's organization,** nor do they help management focus on what is truly important to the customer: quality, responsiveness, production flexibility, dependability, and so forth.

Because everyone uses cost accounting systems, many cost benchmarks are available, giving management a false sense of security. One of the most heavily regulated and cost-analyzed industries, the financial industry, has plenty of cost benchmarks for banking and S&Ls. Still, these did nothing to stop today's problems in the U.S. financial industry. "Comfort in numbers" often covers up the fact that management doesn't understand processes.

Finally, **costs are not "pure."** Financial information is often distorted by allocations that are at best arbitrary. Worse yet, allocations are often the cause of infighting in an organization.

COST MEASURES

As already discussed in Chapter 2, cost information can be of three types and have three characteristics in management decision making.

Costs do not help management focus on what is truly important to the customer: quality, responsiveness, production flexibility, dependability, and so forth.

- **Financial:** Historical financial information reported according to third-party rules is used as a mechanism for reporting, comparing, and reviewing financial information. In the U.S., examples include generally accepted accounting principles; the regulations of the Defense Contract Audit Agency, which define how costs should be accumulated and reported for inventory purposes; and the regulations of the SEC (Securities and Exchange Commission).
- **Operational:** Financial information is used to run the business on a day-to-day basis. Examples include sales backlog, daily sales, and cash balances.
- **Strategic:** This is the cost information needed to make decisions that will have long-term effects on the company. Examples of strategic cost information include make/buy decisions, target cost analysis, and product cost analysis.

Each of these views of costs has three characteristics that should be kept in mind when measures are developed. These characteristics are the required precision of the measure, how often the measure is done, and the focus of the measure— that is, whether it uses historical, current, or future information.

CHARACTERISTICS OF COST INFORMATION

	FINANCIAL	OPERATIONAL	STRATEGIC
REQUIRED PRECISION	Low	High	Low
TIMING	Monthly/ Yearly	Daily	Occasionally
FOCUS	Historical	Actual/ Current	Future

By measuring only financial data, companies automatically court trouble. When it comes to precision, for example, we've seen members of management argue over the fourth decimal, yet not be able to account for quality problems. The issue of timing is just as important. Most companies close their books at the end of the month to inspect quality into their financial processes. A financial view with its historical orientation fails to provide management the right focus, either for the control of daily operations or for future planning. It's a little like driving while looking through the rearview mirror.

Strategic Costs: An example is activity-based costing. Activity-based costing is an analysis of the cost to produce a product, serve the customer, or serve a specific market. Activity-based costing takes a company's costs and attributes them based on the consumption of cost drivers or resources (see Chapter 8).

Operational Costs: An example is a department store's knowledge of sales per square foot by department, used to monitor and receive feedback on merchandising strategies, or the information provided by point-of-purchase cash registers. As the service cycle time is shortened, financial operational information is more important and useful.

In manufacturing companies, because of the comparatively long cycles, daily financial information is not always relevant. However, even manufacturers can use daily operating financial information to drive performance. For example, if one area is consuming a great deal of supplies or producing a lot of waste and rework, it is often a very powerful message to post the daily dollar amounts of those problems in order to draw everyone's attention to the financial impact.

Financial Costs: Examples include the traditional financial general ledger systems, and monthly or annual profit and loss financial statements. Companies need to move from financial information to an operational view and, finally, to the use of strategic costs. That does not mean that management can abandon the financial paradigm. Financial reporting is required by outside third parties, such as the Internal Revenue Service and the Securities and Exchange Commission. But to be appropriate, the information need not be extremely precise. And its timing is very predictable; companies know when the reports are due. With those characteristics in mind, companies can simplify the processes that provide the financial cost information, and thereby meet users' needs efficiently and effectively.

NEW COST ACCOUNTING

In flexible environments that use technology to make a wide variety of products, direct labor becomes less of a factor in the overall cost of a product or process, while indirect, overhead departments and activities drive costs. As "support" functions off the factory floor become more important, management has to get a better handle on them in order to account for and control the company's true costs.

Yet, current costing techniques still allocate overhead as if direct labor were 40 to 50 percent of a product's cost rather than the 5 to 10 percent it is in many industries. Worse yet, the same techniques allocate overhead based on volume consumption rules. The subsequent cost structure is simply no longer meaningful.

Conventional cost accounting systems focus on inventory valuation and financial reporting (rather than on strategic and operational information), track historical variances (including labor efficiency and rate, material price, material usage, fixed and variable spending, overhead fixed volume, and variable efficiency), and highlight inventory levels and turnovers as well as product mix and yield.

But conventional cost accounting systems do **not** support continuous improvement, since standard costs, historical data, and variance reporting do not identify **causes** of costs. Nor do they support flexibility, innovation, or customer satisfaction.

A "new" cost management system would help management do the following:

- **Identify and control overhead costs** (including those generated by such departments and functions as engineering, maintenance, shipping, and purchasing) at department and cost-center levels. Cost allocations would be reduced or eliminated, while costs that do not add value to the product (such as wasted space, material handling, engineering change orders, scrap and rework) could be identified and controlled.
- **Operate with less transaction and variance reporting** and, ideally, manage and track costs in a factory where there are minimal physical inventory counts, minimal work-in-process inventory, minimal hard-copy reports on receiving and shipping, and minimal paper purchase orders.
- **Control cost and productivity through new performance criteria** (such as setup time, production schedules, inventory levels and velocity, space utilization, and team labor) **and** motivate labor without traditional labor efficiency reporting or the measurement of individual work rates.

Conventional cost accounting systems do not support continuous improvement, flexibility, innovation, or customer satisfaction.

- **Make pricing and investment decisions over the entire life cycle of the product.** Measures would be strategic and operational, not just financial. The factory floor would relay timely reports (financial and nonfinancial) to the right people.

QUALITY AND TIME OUTPUT PERFORMANCE MEASURES

Management is comfortable with cost output performance measures because they have been used for many years. The same cannot be said of performance measures for quality and time. But strong trends are pushing the expectations about quality and time. What criteria are included? What criteria will become the most widely accepted?

QUALITY

To set quality output performance measures, companies need standards such as those found in [the Malcolm Baldrige National Quality Award and ISO 9000].

Quality is critical to the survival of organizations. To repeat, quality means understanding, accepting, meeting, and exceeding the wants and expectations of customers continuously. Several new sets of criteria are emerging in industry that define what these characteristics mean in measurement systems. Two new sets of criteria for quality are the Malcolm Baldrige National Quality Award and ISO 9000. When beginning to set output performance measures, companies need standards such as those found in these criteria.

The **Malcolm Baldrige National Quality Award** establishes seven categories for measuring quality. (See Figure 7.2). The following descriptions are from the 1992 award criteria.

FIGURE 7.2
**BALDRIGE AWARD
CRITERIA FRAMEWORK**
From 1992 Award Criteria. Used with permission.

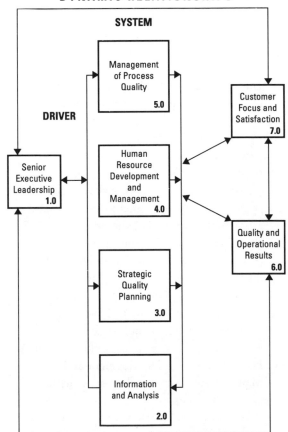

DYNAMIC RELATIONSHIPS

SYSTEM

DRIVER

Management of Process Quality **5.0**

Customer Focus and Satisfaction **7.0**

Senior Executive Leadership **1.0**

Human Resource Development and Management **4.0**

Quality and Operational Results **6.0**

Strategic Quality Planning **3.0**

Information and Analysis **2.0**

GOAL	MEASURES OF PROGRESS
• Customer Satisfaction	• Product and Service Quality
• Customer Satisfaction Relative to Competitors	• Internal Quality and Productivity
• Market Share	• Supplier Quality

1.0 **Senior Executive Leadership** stresses senior executives' **personal** leadership and involvement in creating and sustaining a customer focus and clear and visible quality values. Also examined is how the quality values are integrated into the company's management system and reflected in the manner in which the company addresses its public responsibilities.

2.0 **Information and Analysis** examines the scope, validity, analysis, management, and use of data and information to drive quality excellence and improve competitive performance. Also examined is the adequacy of the company's data, information, and analysis system to support improvement of the company's customer focus, products, services, and internal operations.

3.0 **Strategic Quality Planning** examines the company's planning process and how all key quality requirements are integrated into overall business planning. Also examined are the company's short- and longer-term plans and how quality and performance requirements are deployed to all work units.

4.0 **Human Resource Development and Management** examines the key elements of how the company develops and realizes the full potential of the work force to pursue the company's quality and performance objectives. Also examined are the company's efforts to build and maintain an environment for quality excellence conducive to full participation and personal and organizational growth.

5.0 **Management of Process Quality** examines the systematic process the company uses to pursue ever-higher quality and company performance. Examined are the key elements of process management, including design, management of process quality for all work units and suppliers, systematic quality improvement, and quality assessment.

6.0 **Quality and Operational Results** examines the company's quality levels and improvement trends in quality, company operational performance, and supplier quality. Also examined are current quality and performance levels relative to those of competitors.

7.0 **Customer Focus and Satisfaction** examines the company's relationships with customers and its knowledge of customer requirements and of the key quality factors that determine marketplace competitiveness. Also examined are the company's methods to determine customer satisfaction, current trends and levels of satisfaction, and these results relative to competitors.

The criteria focus on how well a company achieves the following results:

- Customer satisfaction
- Customer satisfaction relative to competitors
- Market share

- Customer indicators such as complaints and customer retention
- Market responsiveness and cycle time
- Product and service quality
- Internal quality, productivity, waste reduction, and asset utilization
- Company-specific effectiveness indicators such as new markets, new technology, and new products
- Supplier quality and supplier development
- Environmental quality, occupational safety and health, and regulatory compliance
- Employee development, well-being, and satisfaction
- National and community well-being

ISO 9000, developed by the International Organization for Standardization, is a set of five international standards for quality management and quality assurance that have been adopted by more than 50 countries. ISO 9000 was created to help companies effectively document their quality system elements. The following excerpts are adapted from ISO 9000 standard ANSI/ASQC Q91-1987.

ISO 9000 consists of 20 elements:

1. **Management Responsibility.** The company's management shall define and document its policy and objectives for, and commitment to, quality. The company shall ensure that

ANSI/ASQC Q91-1987 reprinted with the permission of ASQC (pp. 2-7). Tel: 1-800-248-1946.

this policy is understood, implemented, and maintained at all levels in the organization.

The responsibility, authority, and the interrelation of all personnel who manage, perform, and verify work affecting quality shall be defined.

The company shall identify in-house verification requirements, provide adequate resources, and assign trained personnel for verification activities.

The company shall appoint a management representative who, irrespective of other responsibilities, shall have defined authority and responsibility for ensuring that the requirements of ISO 9000 are implemented and maintained.

The quality system adopted to satisfy the requirements of ISO 9000 shall be reviewed at appropriate intervals by the supplier's management to ensure its continuing suitability and effectiveness. Records of such reviews shall be maintained.

2. **Quality System.** The company shall establish and maintain a documented quality system as a means of ensuring that product conforms to specified requirements.

3. **Contract Review.** The supplier shall establish and maintain procedures for contract review and for the coordination of these activities.

4. **Design Control.** The company shall establish
   and maintain procedures to control and
   verify the design of the product in order
   to ensure that the specified requirements
   are met.
5. **Document Control.** The company shall
   establish and maintain procedures to control
   all documents and data that relate to the
   requirements of this Standard. These
   documents shall be reviewed and approved for
   adequacy by authorized personnel prior to issue.
6. **Purchasing.** The company shall ensure that
   purchased product conforms to specified
   requirements.
7. **Purchaser-Supplied Product.** The company
   shall establish and maintain procedures for
   verification, storage, and maintenance of the
   purchaser-supplied product provided for
   incorporation into the supplies. Any such
   product that is lost, damaged, or is otherwise
   unsuitable for use shall be recorded and
   reported to the purchaser.
8. **Product Identification and Traceability.** Where
   appropriate, the supplier shall establish and
   maintain procedures for identifying the product
   from applicable drawings, specifications, or other
   documents during all stages of production,
   delivery, and installation.

   Where, and to the extent that, traceability
   is a specified requirement, individual product
   or batches shall have a unique identification.
   This identification shall be recorded.

9. **Process Control.** The company shall identify and plan the production and, where applicable, installation processes which directly affect quality and shall ensure that these processes are carried out under controlled conditions.

10. **Inspection and Testing.** The company shall ensure that incoming product is not used or processed **until** it has been inspected or otherwise verified as conforming to specified requirements. Verification shall be in accordance with the quality plan or documented procedures.

11. **Inspection, Measuring, and Test Equipment.** The company shall control, calibrate, and **maintain** inspection, measuring, and test equipment, whether owned by the company, on loan, or provided by the purchaser, to demonstrate the conformance of product to the specified requirements. Equipment shall be used in a manner which ensures that measurement uncertainty is known and is consistent with the required measurement capability.

12. **Inspection and Test Status.** The inspection and test status of product shall be identified by using markings, authorized stamps, tags, labels, routing cards, inspection records, test software, physical location, or other suitable means which indicate the conformance or nonconformance of product with regard to inspection and tests performed.

The identification of inspection and test status shall be maintained, as necessary, throughout production and installation of the product to ensure that only product that has passed the required inspections and tests is dispatched, used, or installed. Records shall identify the inspection authority responsible for the release of conforming product.

13. **Control of Nonconforming Product.**
The company shall establish and maintain procedures to ensure that product that does not conform to specified requirements is prevented from inadvertent use or installation. Control shall provide for identification, documentation, evaluation, segregation when practical, disposition of nonconforming product, and for notification to the functions concerned.

14. **Corrective Action.** The company shall establish, document, and maintain procedures for:

   a) investigating the cause of nonconforming product and the corrective action needed to prevent recurrence;

   b) analyzing all processes, work operations, concessions, quality records, service reports, and customer complaints to detect and eliminate potential causes of nonconforming product;

   c) initiating preventive actions to deal with problems to a level corresponding to the risks encountered;

   d) applying controls to ensure that corrective actions are taken and that they are effective;

e) implementing and recording changes in
procedures resulting from corrective action.

15. **Handling, Storage, Packing, and Delivery.**
The company shall establish, document, and
maintain procedures for handling, storage,
packaging, and delivery of product.

16. **Quality Records.** The company shall establish
and maintain procedures for identification,
collection, indexing, filing, storage,
maintenance, and disposition of quality records.

17. **Internal Quality Audits.** The company shall
carry out a comprehensive system of planned
and documented internal quality audits to
verify whether quality activities comply with
planned arrangements and to determine the
effectiveness of the quality system.

18. **Training.** The company shall establish
and maintain procedures for identifying the
training needs and provide for the training of
all personnel performing activities affecting
quality. Personnel performing specific
assigned tasks shall be qualified on the basis
of appropriate education, training, and/or
experience, as required. Appropriate records
of training shall be maintained.

19. **Servicing.** Where servicing is specified
in the contract, the company shall establish
and maintain procedures for performing
and verifying that servicing meets the
specified requirements.

20. **Statistical Techniques.** Where appropriate,
the company shall establish procedures for

identifying adequate statistical techniques required for verifying the acceptability of process capability and product characteristics.

Companies must have performance measures that measure whether or not they are understanding, accepting, meeting, and exceeding the wants and expectations of their customers continuously— the "goodness" of the product or service. These performance measures are shown in the cell of organization-level quality category, which includes empathy, productivity, reliability, credibility, and competence. In order to develop performance measures that drive a company to quantum performance, it is necessary that companies develop their standards and criteria of quality.

TIME

New standards are also emerging for time as a quantum performance measurement. Here are a few principles:

1. Management must be committed and drive process improvement.
2. Quality must be built in at the source and at every step of the process: "Do it right the first time."
3. Flexibility of the process should be increased through setup reduction and multiple tasking of people and equipment.
4. Companies should produce to demand, not to budget or to inventory.
5. Better relationships with customers and suppliers (both internal and external) improve

a company's understanding of their wants and expectations.

6. The focus is the process; the process path should be kept short and simple. Simplification is the key.

For years Motorola set the standard for lead time in the delivery of pagers. The time from placement of an order until a pager was shipped was 40 days. The pager had over 1,000 parts.

Then Motorola implemented Six Sigma, its total quality management process. The company reengineered the way its pagers are made and set a new standard in lead time. Today, that same type of pager has only 100 parts. When you pick up the phone to order a pager, it will be shipped one hour and forty minutes later. Motorola does not even begin to manufacture a pager until an order is received. Still they can produce it in an hour and forty minutes.

To survive, companies must have processes that are not only fast, but are also flexible to change. Time output performance measures allow an organization to gauge its ability to respond to shifting customer demand patterns and its willingness to change—the "goodness" of its process. (See Chapter 2 for a discussion of the output performance measures of velocity, flexibility, responsiveness, and resilience.)

Time output performance measures allow an organization to gauge its ability to respond to shifting customer demand patterns and its willingness to change.

SETTING OUTPUT PERFORMANCE MEASURES

Companies need output performance measures that address cost, quality, and time because they have to manage the expectations of the customers (quality), the demands on their processes (time), and the economics of the organization (cost)— all at the same time.

ACTION STEPS: DEVELOPING OUTPUT PERFORMANCE MEASURES

Following are the steps for designing and developing output performance measures:

1. **Identify the customers of the process.** It is necessary to know who the internal and external customers are. This is obviously important since the output performance measures are used to report the result of the process, and it is necessary to know whether the output is what customers want.
2. **Identify and understand customers' expectations.**
3. **Filter and prioritize these expectations.** This can be performed more easily after developing an understanding of the customers of the process and what their expectations are. The goals of the organization will assist you as well.
4. **Select the performance measures that link the process to the goals to the customers.** Use the

Matrix as a guide and the cost, quality and time criteria discussed earlier.

5. **Set targets using benchmark information.**

Setting performance measures is easy once management understands strategy and goals, customer wants, and processes.

VITAL SIGNS

KEY ACTIVITIES

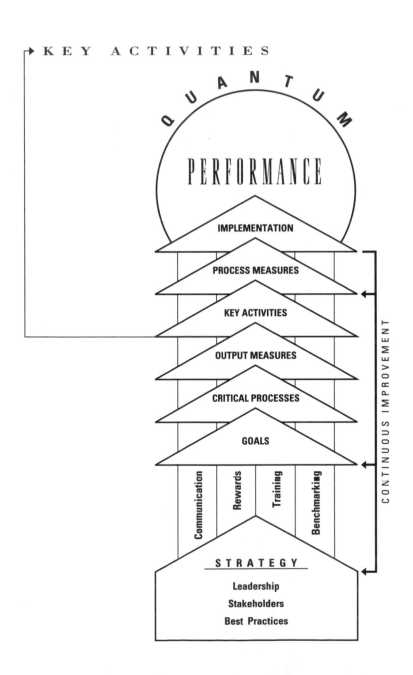

8
KEY
ACTIVITIES

■ DEFINITION

A key activity is a step critical to the integrity
of a process or its output. The primary tool for
understanding processes is process mapping: a visual
representation of the activities, across functions, that
are needed to produce a product or service.

● BENEFITS

Process mapping creates a common basis for focus and
communication, as well as identifying opportunities for
process simplification.

▲ RISKS

Traditionally, companies have been functionally
segmented, and management has been
transaction-focused.

A key activity is a step critical to the integrity of a process or its output.

A key activity is a step critical to the integrity of a process or its output. For this reason, it's important that performance measures be set on key activities.

Who should be involved in determining the key activities in a process?

People with knowledge of the process—cross-functional teams—are necessary for determining key activities since processes cut across various functions. Companies also may want to include customers, because they often have a unique view of what's important to the process. Suppliers also may offer unique insights, but they have to have knowledge of the performance measure process. For example, Toyota uses suppliers in new product development and manufacturing because this allows them to understand Toyota's processes and provide important input.

Who decides upon the team?

The manager of the process or the person responsible for the process should decide who is to be a member of the team.

How are key activities identified?

The tools used are consistent with the seven management and planning tools (Chapter 6) and seven basic tools (discussed later in this chapter) used to identify qualitative and quantitative information. The team reaches consensus on key activities. The number of performance measures should be kept as low as possible, and the number of key activities should range between two and six per process in order to keep everyone's attention on what is really important.

The inputs the team uses to identify key activities include a process map (see below), the product definition from the customers, the output performance measures developed in Chapter 7, and the strategies and goals of the organization. The team should identify the key activities that support the product output, strategies, and goals of the organization.

PROCESS MAPPING

The primary tool for understanding processes is process mapping: a visual representation of the activities in various functions in an organization that are needed to produce a product or service. Through process mapping everyone can see when, where, and how to improve processes. Then they can improve the customer focus of the processes, eliminate nonvalue-added activities, and reduce process complexity.

The primary tool for understanding processes is process mapping. Through process mapping everyone can see when, where, and how to improve processes.

Process mapping, in general, requires several steps.

First, identify the product/service and the related processes. This includes choosing "start" and "stop" points so that everyone can agree on the parameters of the process.

Second, document the process through interviews and discussions. No single person in a process understands the whole process.

Many people must contribute their knowledge—alone or in groups—to uncover all the activities in the process.

Third, transfer the information to a visual representation. It's often useful—and necessary—for the team to walk through the process. Look for nonvalue-added activities—bottlenecks, wasted activities, delays, and duplications of efforts—that can be eliminated.

The major goal of process mapping is to create a common basis for focus and communication.

The major goal of process mapping is to create a common basis for focus and communication. Process mapping provides a language through which people can share their understanding. Everyone shares the same paradigm; everyone has the same foundation.

When managers understand processes, they have a solid foundation for improvement. Once a process is documented in a clear and concise format, it's easier to see opportunities for improved responsiveness, quality, or cost reduction. Process mapping opens up a dialogue between management and employees by creating a common understanding of what is really happening in the business. People actually working within a process should define its key activities and devise performance measures for these activities and for the junctures between them. Once customer wants are understood and a strategy is developed to address these wants, process mapping is the first step in developing effective process performance measures.

People actually working within a process should define its key activities and devise performance measures for these activities and for the junctures between them.

In addition, with process mapping, management can see where and why resources are consumed. One manufacturer complained of resource scarcity and poor productivity in engineering. The company was struggling to increase the department's effectiveness, but throwing resources at the problem just made matters worse. Process mapping showed that, in fact, more than 50 percent of the department's activities were nonvalue-added: administrative trivia; budget meetings; and filling simplistic, nonengineering requests from other areas. With this understanding, management was able to act effectively.

Finally, a mapped process is a good basis for training. Typically, companies train new employees on the job without any tools to help them learn. Process documentation enables management to communicate what is really happening in the organization and what should happen in each job. Employees see how their activities fit into larger processes and how these, in turn, focus on meeting and exceeding customer needs, wants, and expectations.

WHY DON'T MORE COMPANIES MAP THEIR PROCESSES?

First, **companies are not organized by processes;** they're organized by functions. Specialization, as espoused by business thinkers such as Frederick Taylor (1911) in the early 1900s, had a simple thesis: The more one performs a task, the better one performs it.

With process mapping, management can see where and why resources are consumed.

This encouraged segmentation into functional silos. All the engineers are in one department, doing only engineering, supervised by other engineers. On the plant floor, all welders are grouped together and do nothing but welding. Financial people, organized into a department, do financial reports over and over and over.

But companies do not serve customers from vertical silos. Customer service crosses all functions, horizontally. In reality, the actual processes required to meet and exceed customers' wants, needs, and expectations are hidden.

Second, **no one is responsible for processes.** Top executives have organizational titles that relate to their functions and specialties, but no one has a process orientation. This sends a message to employees: Management does not care about processes.

Third, because management does not understand the organization's processes, the **processes evolve haphazardly**—without structure, without organization, without management's attention—as a company changes over time. What management thinks is happening on the shop floor or in administrative areas is old news and no longer accurate or relevant. The processes have already changed.

Fourth, **process mapping is hard to do.** In most situations, processes have not been documented, and it's difficult to get started. Process mapping involves working with the details of the organization, the "down and dirty" business of the business. Also, it's easy to get lost in the details of a process.

Traditionally, management has been transaction-focused—sell off a division, open a plant, negotiate a contract. Executives are trained to deal with transactions, but processes are day-in and day-out activities. At the same time, it's important that management understand customers' and suppliers' processes.

It's important that management understand customers' and suppliers' processes.

Being a good vendor means to meet or exceed customers' needs, wants, and expectations. Who are the customers? What do they need? What are their measures and expectations? The answers lie in understanding processes. With these answers, a company can anticipate customers' unexpressed and unknown needs and, by meeting them, build in switching costs.

Being a good customer means getting one's own needs, wants, and expectations fulfilled. What does a vendor value? How can a company help a supplier provide better-quality raw materials? Understanding a supplier's processes shows ways to help eliminate glitches that might be inhibiting satisfaction. Barriers are eliminated, and the whole pipeline functions better.

The importance of understanding processes cannot be overstated—not just one's own processes, but the processes of customers and suppliers up and down the product stream.

SIMPLIFY, SIMPLIFY, SIMPLIFY

Once management knows and understands the company's processes, it can simplify them.

Eliminate unnecessary tasks and activities that do not focus on customer needs, wants, and expectations.

To simplify means to eliminate unnecessary tasks and activities that do not focus on customer needs, wants, and expectations (expressed, unexpressed, or unknown). There are several key principles of simplification.

First, **one must know what is important.** Therefore, one must understand what is valued in a process.

Second, **value is defined by the customer** (external or internal) and by other stakeholders (employees, owners, or investors).

Third, **tasks and activities that do not add value must be eliminated.** These can equal 50 percent— or more—of the activities within a process.

Fourth, **the remaining value-added tasks must be simplified.** Doing so means examining the process path: Can we shorten the process path? Can we prevent lapses of time? Is there any duplication or repetition? Are all the steps necessary? Can any activities be combined? Can automation or new procedures streamline the path? The simplification process questions the "number" of things—number of components, number of copies, number of steps.

Fifth, **processes are enhanced as new, customer-defined values emerge.**

There are warning signs of unnecessary
complexity:

- Labor-intensive processes: Why is so much
  labor required?
- Review cycles: Why is quality inspected in
  rather than built in?
- Duplication: Why are activities—such as
  price checks—performed not once but two,
  three, or four times?
- Delays or bottlenecks: Why are piles of paper
  waiting to be processed? Why is inventory
  queuing before and after manufacturing
  processes?
- Excessive (or any) paperwork: Why is a
  report needed? Can it be eliminated?
- Omissions: What customer values are not
  addressed by the organization's processes?
- Time: Can time in the process path
  be compressed?

FIGURE 8.2
TYPES OF PROCESS MAPS

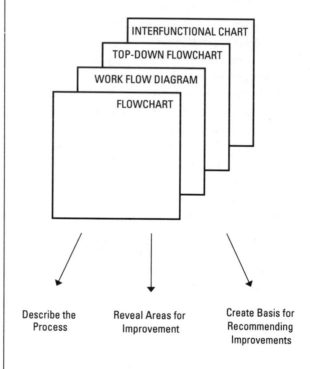

TOOLS AND TECHNIQUES

PROCESS MAPS

There are different types of process maps (Figure 8.2). Each has its good qualities and its drawbacks. To understand a process, a company usually needs two of the following four types of maps:

- Flowchart
- Work flow diagram
- Top-down flowchart
- Interfunctional chart

The **flowchart** (Figure 8.3) is the first type of process map. A flowchart displays a series of actions and decisions. It is easy to understand; it allows companies to document things very quickly. But flowcharts are useful only in very simple processes. With complex processes, flowcharts are very cumbersome, very detailed, and very hard to follow. Most organizations have multiple decisions throughout a process. These decisions are difficult to document in a traditional flowchart.

The second type of process map is the **work flow diagram** (Figure 8.4)—a schematic diagram that traces the flow of the process through the work area. On the plant floor, this type of process map tracks a product through production. In office administration, one can map the work flow in billing, payroll, customer service, or order entry.

Work flow diagrams are often called **spaghetti charts** because of the complexity of the work flow

FIGURE 8.3
FLOWCHART
Reprinted with permission from *The Memory Jogger: A Pocket Guide of Tools for Continuous Improvement.* p. 12. Copyright ©1988 GOAL/QPC, 13 Branch Street, Methuen, MA 01844-1953. Tel: 508-685-3900.

TURNING ON A TELEVISION

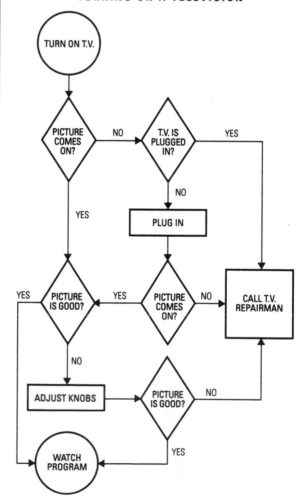

FIGURE 8.4
WORK FLOW DIAGRAM

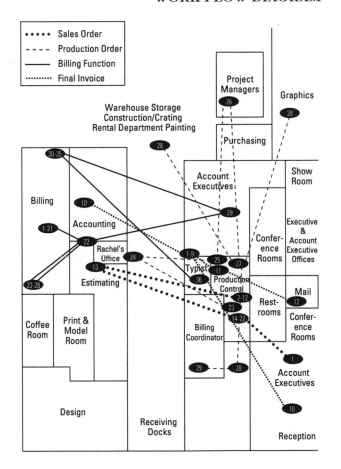

as the product moves through various stations for processing. Work flow diagrams show excessive process paths, bottlenecks, delays, and so forth. They are powerful communication tools because they show so much waste. The weakness of the work flow diagram is that it does not suggest corrections other than a few simple rearrangements.

The third type of process map is the **top-down flowchart** (Figure 8.5). Most processes in organizations are very complex; when process mapping, it's easy to get lost in the details. The top-down flowchart is useful in documenting complex processes and in instilling discipline in process mapping. The top-down flowchart documents the beginning and end of the process; no more than six critical elements, or steps, are documented. Of those six critical elements, the top two or three are selected. Within each, six critical elements are studied.

Three levels deep is usually enough. The top-down process keeps analysts from getting lost in the details. It's also a very powerful tool for designing **new** processes. Top-down flowcharts (like interfunctional charts described next) are not very appealing visually, but help lead to solutions.

The fourth type of process map is the **interfunctional chart** (Figure 8.6). Developed by Geary Rummler and Alan Brache, this powerful tool shows the cross-functionality of a process and demonstrates the weakness in a process during "handoffs." Because cross-functionality must be identified to effect

FIGURE 8.5
TOP-DOWN FLOWCHART

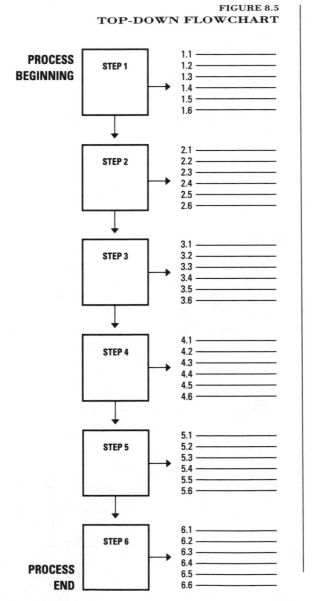

FIGURE 8.6
INTERFUNCTIONAL CHART

GROUPS

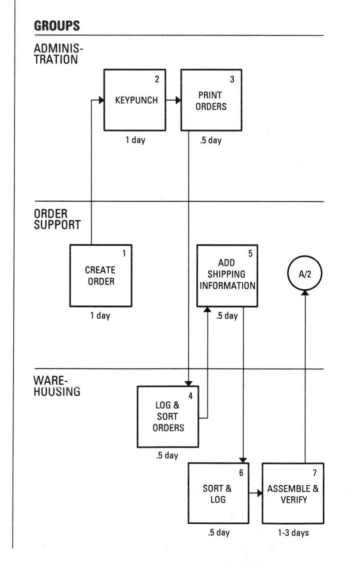

ADMINIS-
TRATION

ORDER
SUPPORT

WARE-
HOUSING

simplification and streamlining, the interfunctional chart is valuable. However, it is not so visually appealing as a work flow diagram and often does not seize management's attention. But a work flow diagram and an interfunctional chart can be a very powerful combination.

FACT GATHERING (SEVEN BASIC TOOLS)

When identifying key activities, management must make decisions based on facts. Seven productivity tools are used in the fact-gathering process. The tools of management fact gathering are described by Michael Brassard in *The Memory Jogger™: A Pocket Guide of Tools for Continuous Improvement*, which should be referred to for details on how to use these tools. These include cause-and-effect diagrams (also called Ishikawa or fishbone diagrams), Pareto charts, histograms, check sheets, run diagrams, and control charts, as well as process maps discussed previously. These are used to capture and analyze **quantitative** data for problem identification and resolution.

CAUSE-AND-EFFECT DIAGRAM

The cause-and-effect diagram (Figure 8.7) is a tool for analyzing the causes of a problem. It is also referred to as the Ishikawa diagram, after developer Kaoru Ishikawa, as well as the fishbone

The tools for continuous improvement adapted with permission from *The Memory Jogger: A Pocket Guide of Tools for Continuous Improvement*. pp. 14, 17, 24-25, 30, 36-37, 44, 51-52. Copyright ©1988 GOAL/QPC, 13 Branch Street, Methuen, MA 01844-1953. Tel: 508-685-3900.

To identify key activities, management must make decisions based on facts.

FIGURE 8.7 CAUSE-AND-EFFECT DIAGRAM

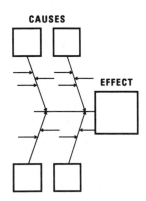

FIGURE 8.8
PARETO CHART

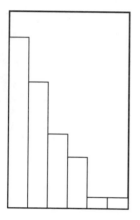

FIGURE 8.9
HISTOGRAM

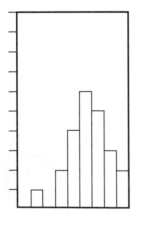

diagram, because the completed diagram resembles a fish skeleton. The diagram illustrates the main causes and subcauses leading to an effect (problem).

This tool is used in small teams to identify causes to a process problem. The problem is written in the square to the right, and the team brainstorms on the problem and writes the causes on the "bones" of the diagram. After problem causes are identified, the team gains consensus on the three to five causes that have the most impact on the problem. Productivity tools are then used to collect qualitative data.

PARETO CHART

A Pareto chart (Figure 8.8) is a graphical tool for ranking causes from the most significant to the least significant. It is based on the Pareto principle. The principle, named after 19th century economist Vilfredo Pareto, suggests that most effects come from relatively few causes; that is, 80 percent of the effects come from 20 percent of the possible causes.

The Pareto chart and the Pareto principle help identify the 20 percent of activities—the key activities in a process—where performance measures should be developed and monitored.

HISTOGRAM

A histogram (Figure 8.9) is a graphic summary of variation in a set of data. The pictorial nature of

Pareto chart and histogram adapted with permission from *The Memory Jogger: A Pocket Guide of Tools for Continuous Improvement.* pp. 17, 36. Copyright ©1988 GOAL/QPC, 13 Branch Street, Methuen, MA 01844-1953. Tel: 508-685-3900.

the histogram lets people see patterns that are difficult to visualize in a simple table of numbers.

Performance measures displayed in a histogram provide a pictorial view of variation.

CHECK SHEET

A check sheet displays how frequently an event occurs. See Figure 8.10.

A check sheet can be used to convince management that a process is causing employees to do the "wrong" thing. For example, the customer service representatives at a small manufacturing company told us that they couldn't serve customers because they were spending most of their time performing secretarial duties for the president and two vice presidents. We shared the customer reps' concern with top management, who said the reps were just lazy and trying to get out of work. Knowing the importance of managing by facts, we asked the reps to list their six most critical activities and another category named "other" across the top of a check sheet and the clock times from 8:00 to 5:00 in 15-minute increments along the side of the sheet. At 8:00, 8:15, and so on, the reps marked the column that coincided with the activity that they were engaged in. After two weeks, the check sheets

FIGURE 8.10
CHECK SHEET

A	B	C	D	E	Total
I	I		I		3
II		I		II	5
I	I		III		5
	I		I	I	3
III	I	III			7
	I		I	I	3
II	II	II	II	II	10

Check sheet and scatter diagram (on next page) adapted with permission from *The Memory Jogger: A Pocket Guide of Tools for Continuous Improvement.* pp. 14, 44. Copyright ©1988 GOAL/QPC, 13 Branch Street, Methuen, MA 01844-1953. Tel: 508-685-3900.

FIGURE 8.11
SCATTER
DIAGRAM

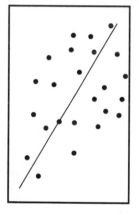

showed that the reps spent 60 percent of their time performing activities in the "other" category. Based on this data, top management hired two secretaries.

SCATTER DIAGRAM

A scatter diagram is a graphical technique for analyzing the relationship between two variables. As shown in Figure 8.11, two sets of data are plotted on a graph, with the Y axis being used for the variable to be predicted and the X axis being used for the variable to make the prediction. The graph will show possible relationships. (Although two variables might appear to be related, they might not be—those who know most about the variable must make that evaluation.)

A scatter diagram can be used to chart the relationship between the number of skills that a person has and the number of defects in products produced.

CONTROL CHART

A control chart (Figure 8.12) is a chart with upper and lower control limits on which values of some statistical measure for a series of samples or subgroups are plotted. The chart frequently shows a central line to help detect a trend of plotted values toward either control limit.

A variation of this tool, called the run chart, is used in the service industries. As shown in Figure 8.13, a run chart represents data visually by plotting points on the graph in the order in which the information they represent becomes available. Run charts are used to monitor a process to

FIGURE 8.12
CONTROL CHART

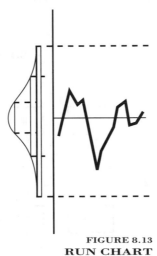

FIGURE 8.13
RUN CHART

Control chart and run chart adapted with permission from *The Memory Jogger: A Pocket Guide of Tools for Continuous Improvement.* pp. 30, 52. Copyright ©1988 GOAL/QPC, 13 Branch Street, Methuen, MA 01844-1953. Tel: 508-685-3900.

**FIGURE 8.14
PROCESS MAP
(WORK FLOW DIAGRAM)**

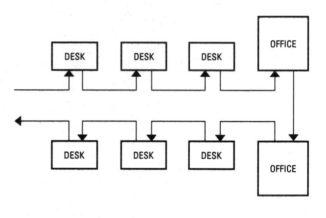

BEFORE...

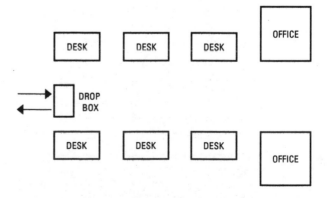

AFTER...

determine if the long-range average is changing. It is common to graph the results of a process such as machine downtime, yield, scrap, typographical errors, or productivity as they vary over time.

PROCESS MAP

The seventh tool, the process map, has been discussed earlier in this chapter. However, it is important to discuss its further importance.

In addition to the benefits discussed previously, we have used this tool to build camaraderie and encourage teamwork. For cross-functional teams whose members traditionally do not work with one another, mapping the steps in a process usually increases understanding and empathy. Comments like "I didn't know you did all that" or "Maybe we shouldn't do that any more" are common.

Some of the Seven Basic Tools are more useful than others. The cause-and-effect diagram, for example, is excellent for determining **why** things occur, while the process map is perhaps best for documenting **how** things occur.

All these tools and techniques have been around for a long time. The problem is that they are not widely used outside of small groups. Why?

- People think these are manufacturing tools, not applicable elsewhere.
- People are not trained in the use of these tools, or are not experienced in their use.
- Too few people are involved. Process mapping requires cross-functional cooperation. The

A process map may be used to build camaraderie and encourage teamwork.

more views of a process, the better. Even though group discussions are important for the ideas they generate, most U.S. companies do not commonly use teams or groups to perform tasks or resolve problems.

- People don't really want the facts. They'd prefer to make decisions based on history or "gut feel."

Example: To improve its company's billing process, management asked a simple question: Who is the customer of the billing process? Then a cross-functional team—including people within the process (billing), people in functions (such as production) outside the process, and management —was established to find the answers.

The team's first discovery was a discrepancy in perceptions. Initially, the billing department clerks listed four customers. At the end of the interview/ discussion phase, they listed eight. It was clear that billing didn't know who its customers were.

Next, the team asked billing to define its customers' needs, wants, and expectations. Through affinity diagrams and focus groups, the team drew two conclusions: Many things that billing thought customers wanted, they didn't; and many things customers did want, billing did not provide.

Finally, the team mapped the process and found out that preparing a bill required 59 days and 275 different steps. The bill traveled approximately two miles during the process.

The visual representation, with its twists and turns, surprised everyone. More than 50 percent of the activities—rechecking, recalculating, reworking—had no relationship to the customer. Once this was clear, so was the fact that, without process improvement, performance improvement was impossible.

ACTIVITY-BASED COSTING

One derivative from process mapping—activity-based costing (ABC)—is gaining popularity as a way to identify resources consumed based on processes. ABC allocates and directs overhead costs to activities rather than using allocations based on direct labor, machine hours, material costs, and so forth. For this reason, ABC can do a good job of capturing reliable product costs, product line costs, or customer costs.

Activity-based costing [is] a way to identify resources consumed based on processes.

THE BENEFITS OF ABC

Activity-based costing has a number of benefits. First, ABC **answers management's key questions:** "What are our costs? Where should we focus efforts to control cost? What activities or events are driving our costs? What will information about the costs of our products and processes do for us in the market? If we understand our product costs better, how can we use that knowledge to enhance our market position?"

This information supports decision making, since ABC requires an understanding of processes and cost drivers. Is a product profitable? Should a product be discontinued? Should it be priced, marketed, or distributed differently? While the answers depend on more than cost structures, an accurate knowledge of costs influences performance plans, targets, and measurement.

Second, ABC **supports a customer focus** by helping a company measure and manage two types of activities: value-added (those that enhance customer satisfaction) and nonvalue-added (those that should be reduced and/or eliminated).

Third, ABC **supports "core competence."** It's not about financial numbers; rather, it is grounded in the actual work people do to make a product or deliver a service. The performance measures that "fall out" of ABC help the plant or office solve problems, not account for them, by focusing on the efficient use of resources to put out a good product for an acceptable price.

Fourth, ABC **generates more complete and, therefore, more reliable costing information.** Companies have a clearer knowledge of whether a product or service is actually profitable. By getting cost accounting and management off the shop floor, ABC analysis includes everything from order entry and design engineering through marketing and logistics. The broader the scope, the more valuable the analysis, especially since as much as 80 percent of a product's final cost is "designed in" before actual manufacturing begins.

Fifth, ABC **helps identify costs and activities that can be minimized or eliminated** because

ABC pinpoints cost drivers in the total product order-to-delivery cycle. And it helps improve and manage processes. Since ABC requires an understanding of processes, it stands to reason that it can be a first step toward process improvement.

Because its information is historical, ABC provides a "snapshot" view of costs for a single period of time. So, the true value of ABC is what management does with the information once it's been generated. If it's not used to drive out costs, ABC can become just another way to report "the numbers." The key advantage of ABC is that it provides a more accurate way to look at overhead and indirect costs, including those generated off the factory floor and not typically factored into product-by-product cost calculations—activities such as marketing, distribution, and maintenance.

ABC: STEP BY STEP

There are five basic steps in conducting activity-based costing.

First, **determine product lines.** This may sound simple, but companies often take either too narrow or too broad an approach. Some want to divide their products into two or three different lines (making ABC impossible), while others want to spread costs over thousands of products or SKUs (which is just as bad).

It's necessary to ask some simple questions. "Why are we doing ABC? What decisions will be made based on the information?" With answers, it's easier to determine product lines.

The true value of ABC is what management does with the information once it's been generated.

The key advantage of ABC is that it provides a more accurate way to look at overhead and indirect costs.

Second, **understand the processes** behind the product lines, starting with the products and moving back through the organization. Identify the necessary activities, not just in manufacturing, but in the whole business-cycle pipeline.

Third, **select important processes—from a customer viewpoint**—and analyze the costs in those processes. Again, the entire pipeline of activities should be included in the analysis. Limiting the scope only reduces the effectiveness of ABC, since some of the biggest benefits can be achieved off the factory floor in support and white-collar areas.

Fourth, **attribute costs based on the consumption of resources.** How are costs attributed? How are the rules for consumption determined? By interviewing people and reviewing the processes to find out how and why activities are initiated.

Then, these causes (cost drivers) have to be traced back to particular products. How are resources consumed? The rules should be determined based on the usage of resources in each product category.

Fifth, **develop a product-line cost model,** using a future focus to support strategic information with the intent of understanding not just what costs were but what they will be.

ABC helps management identify value-added tasks and activities within a process.

Done the right way, ABC helps management identify value-added tasks and activities within a process. By eliminating the nonvalue-added tasks and activities, management can initiate change and reduce costs. Activity-based costing links resources to processes to products to customers and markets.

With ABC (as with any other management tool), results are most satisfactory if management has appropriate expectations and an accurate appreciation of what the technique can do and how to use it most effectively.

In reality, fixed costs do not disappear just because ABC might indicate that a product is unprofitable and ripe for dropping. While ABC might say, "This product is unprofitable; therefore, discontinue it," other strategic questions have to be considered:

- Must the product be part of the company's line because it's part of a family? If a company makes batteries, for example, it can hardly choose to drop the AAA size, even if that were not as profitable as the C size.
- Is the product part of the company's long-term objectives? Making a maximum profit in the short term is not necessarily in the best interests of survival over time. ABC is a valuable tool, and the information it generates about product costs and the activities behind them can be very useful in strategic decision making. But, to take full advantage of ABC to promote continuous improvement, management must analyze the information with a view toward overall business processes.

The information that comes out of the Model during the key activities stage should support

Information from the key activities stage should support the simplification of processes, the elimination of nonvalue-added activities, a companywide focus on strategic objectives, and customer satisfaction.

the simplification of processes, the elimination of nonvalue-added activities, a companywide focus on strategic objectives, and customer satisfaction.

FIND THE COST DRIVERS

Activity-based costing attributes costs directly to products, so that costs that do not add value to the product can be eliminated. Identifying these costs is not enough; management also has to understand what's **causing** the nonvalue-added costs. These causes often include the following:

- **Product design,** including material specifications, types of materials, the quality of materials, the complexity of the design, the number of operations required to make the product, and the durability of tooling
- **Process design,** including repair processing, inspection procedures, amount of uptime, setup time, material handling, and the ease of maintaining equipment
- **Sourcing and logistics,** including the price of material, the capability of vendors, scrap in vendor products, freight costs to and from the plant, containers, inventory buffers, the scheduling process, the amount of expediting, and the purchasing process
- **Organization,** including worker absenteeism, levels of supervision and management, administrative activities, and indirect support in the plant, such as maintenance, quality control, and training.

ABC: THE RIGHT WAY

- Attribute costs to activities that drive them. If, for example, the primary cost driver is the number of parts on a master part list, then the product with the most parts gets more costs, as opposed to costs being spread evenly or not spread at all.
- Get out of the financial department and learn about processes. Look at cost drivers throughout the whole organization and pipeline, including preproduction and postproduction activities. These costs are often ignored by traditional cost accounting.

ABC: THE WRONG WAY

- Identify too many cost drivers. Hundreds of allocations make the measurement system just as complex, difficult to use, confusing, and arbitrary as today's cost accounting.
- Use ABC to run the business. ABC is not an operational tool—it's a strategic one. ABC does not replace financial or operational systems. As a strategic measurement, ABC should have the appropriate characteristics: low precision, timing on demand (ABC is not a mainline system), and a future focus on customer or market profitability.
- Use ABC from the top down, from the general ledger to products. Called the

"rack and stack" method of ABC, shifting numbers in the ledger provides no new information. Rather, ABC begins with an understanding of processes. Once processes and activities are understood, costs can be directed to products or customers or markets, based on what's causing the activities.

VITAL SIGNS

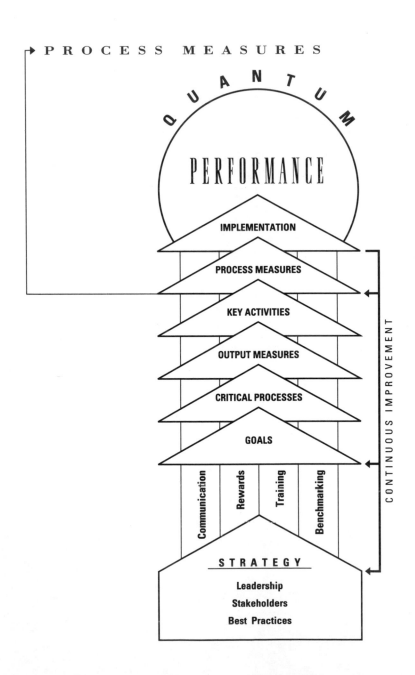

PROCESS MEASURES

QUANTUM

PERFORMANCE

IMPLEMENTATION

PROCESS MEASURES

KEY ACTIVITIES

OUTPUT MEASURES

CRITICAL PROCESSES

GOALS

Communication   Rewards   Training   Benchmarking

STRATEGY

Leadership

Stakeholders

Best Practices

CONTINUOUS IMPROVEMENT

9

PROCESS PERFORMANCE MEASURES

■ **DEFINITION**

Process performance measures report the activities of the process and motivate people to control the process.

● **BENEFITS**

Process measures enable management to monitor progress, anticipate and prevent problems, continuously improve the process, verify the selection of key activities, and motivate people.

▲ **RISKS**

Without process measures, people within the processes have no way to improve them. Process measures must be actionable: People must be able to control them.

While cost measures are generally used as a management tool, cost also can be a process performance measure. In a manufacturing environment, for example, tool fixtures are very expensive. One company was having problems with the setup and the sharpening of a milling machine. Instead of just keeping track of the number of bits that were broken as a process performance measure, the company recorded the cost incurred: $5,000 every time a bit was broken. This was more powerful than simply keeping track of bits. In that case, cost was used as a process performance measure.

In another example, everyone at NUMMI (New United Motor Manufacturing Inc.) in Fremont, California, is encouraged to stop the line when there are problems. However, everyone also knows that stopping the line costs $8,000 a minute, which is recorded as the balance cost performance measure at the process level.

For a performance measure to be effective, people in the process must be able to control the measure.

As already mentioned, for a performance measure to be effective, the people in the process must be able to control the measure. Often the people in the process have very little control over budget or cost. In the examples above, though, the people in the process have direct responsibility and direct control over costs. If the drill bit in the first example is not set up right or if it's not maintained right, then it usually breaks. At NUMMI, the workers can stop the line. Therefore, it makes sense to include the cost of that action as a process performance measure. However, when the people in the process have no control over costs, using cost to monitor performance is demotivating.

NUMMI is balancing the categories of performance measures. Quality is obviously the overriding concern because the company wants to produce cars with 100 percent quality, all the time. Because the workers have to balance the cost when the quality is not right, and because stopping the line incurs additional costs to correct quality, operators are driven to build in quality instead of inspecting in quality. And, operators must continuously balance cost and velocity in controlling their performance measures. If they stop the line, production is slowed down; they're not producing on schedule.

After selecting the key activities of the process, the Performance Measurement Team should develop and select the process performance measures. Again, process performance measures report the activities of the process and motivate people to control the process. As we discussed earlier, it's important to have process performance measures to give the performance measurement system balance.

Process performance measures report the activities of the process and motivate people to control the process.

Process performance measures do five things.

First, they **monitor progress.** Performance measures should be set so that the people within the process know quickly whether the process is improving or if it is still in control. Among the performance measures used to monitor progress are traditional manufacturing measures such as statistical process control. Also included are performance measures such as length of process path, which is often used to focus on decreasing the length of the process path, thereby continuously improving the process.

Second, process performance measures **anticipate and prevent problems.** Since these measures monitor and control key activities, the people in the process are able to prevent problems— and solve problems after they occur. Examples of performance measures that allow people to anticipate and prevent problems include statistical process control and clerical accuracy checks on key activities in an office environment.

Process performance measures focus people on continuous improvement.

Third, process performance measures **continuously improve the process.** Since companies must continuously improve to stay competitive, all the people in a process must strive for continuous improvement. Process performance measures focus people on continuous improvement.

Tracking the number of activities in a process is one example of a performance measure that helps organizations improve continuously. As the people within the process continuously decrease the number of activities, the elapsed time of the process typically decreases, quality increases, and costs come down.

Measuring the process path is another way to continuously improve process performance. As the process is organized and the process path decreases (which reduces space), the people within the process can manage by sight as opposed

to managing by reporting. They can spot
problems quickly.

Inventory levels are also used as a performance
measure to continuously improve the process.
When people strive to reduce inventories within
the process, they do more than improve the cost
structure of the organization; they also expose
quality problems previously hidden in stocks
of inventory.

Fourth, process performance measures **verify the
selection of key activities.** When companies begin
developing and implementing performance
measures, they often do not understand all the
activities within each process. Therefore, their first
attempt at identifying key processes might not be
completely reliable. Having process performance
measures on key activities, and monitoring these
measures, allows people to know if they have
chosen correctly. If the activities improve but the
integrity of the process or output does not as
measured by the output performance measures,
then the activity that has been selected is not a key
activity. This selection process is important because
people cannot monitor everything. Attention must
be focused on key activities that are crucial to the
integrity of the process and output.

As the process continuously improves and
changes, key activities also may change. What
is important at one time may differ from what's
important later on. And process performance
measures have to change to address new

*As the process
continuously improves
and changes, key
activities also may
change, impacting
process performance
measures.*

activities that become key as the process matures. For example, an organization may have a problem with the receipt of raw material from vendors. Therefore, a key activity may be verifying the quality of incoming raw materials. Through vendor certification (which includes decreasing the number and improving the quality of the vendors), the receiving company should not have to check the incoming quality of the raw materials. Then that activity can be eliminated.

Process performance measures should focus on improving the process, not on criticizing people.

Fifth, process performance measures **motivate people.** Performance measures posted at the work site give people a score and motivate them to do better. People always want to know how they are doing. Giving them a score to aim for is, in itself, motivational. Process performance measures should focus on improving the process, not on criticizing people. Performance is a process issue, not a people issue. Therefore, motivation comes from directing the performance measures at improving the process and its results.

SETTING AND IMPLEMENTING PROCESS PERFORMANCE MEASURES

There are six key steps in setting and implementing process performance measures.

First, **go back to the goals of the organization,** which reveal what the people within the process should focus on and achieve through the process. It is important that the goals of the organization remain the driving force when determining the process performance measures.

Second, **go to the Matrix and determine the categories of measurement.** On the Matrix, people measures are always process measures. The process-level measures can be either process or output measures. For this reason, it's important that companies look at both the process and the people levels of the Matrix. In addition, depending on the goals of the organization, management may want to focus on a specific category in the Matrix: cost, quality, or time. Since companies have multiple goals, they need to balance their performance measures, making sure to look at the right level and the right category.

Third, with the criteria of cost, quality, and time as discussed in Chapter 7, **select within the Matrix the types of performance measures that support the goals.** Again, the types of performance measures include such things as reliability, responsiveness, flexibility, and compensation. After developing an understanding of the goals of the organization and the cost, quality and time criteria and also looking at the key activities within the processes, it's possible to identify the appropriate process performance measures. If the key activity is people-sensitive or people-dependent, the people category is appropriate. If time is an important constraint, responsiveness or resilience would be good measures. If, on the other hand, quality is an overriding goal of the organization, the conformance or productivity measure would be critical.

Fourth, once the proper performance measure or measures are chosen, **determine what to measure and how to measure it.** Frequently, performance measures are too complex and difficult to understand. It is much better if the people within the process understand what they're measuring and why. If these people can relate the measurement back to the goals of the organization, the performance measure is valid.

Process performance measures do not have to be reported up and down the organization. They are used by the people within the process.

Many companies find the collection of performance measures so cumbersome that the efforts collapse under their own weight, so how to measure is also very important. Process performance measures do not have to be reported up and down the organization. The performance measures are used to monitor progress, to prevent problems, improve the process, and so forth. That means they are used by the people within the process. Measuring and reporting performance measures within the process doesn't necessarily require fancy computer systems or multicopy reports. Often process performance measures can be reported through old-fashioned cell display boards or by posting the performance measure over the key activity itself.

Fifth, **determine whether the performance measure is an attribute or a variable measure.** The difference is that attributes derive from yes/no questions, whereas variable measures involve a range of measurement. Attribute measures can be used in key activities that are under control. It is necessary to be alerted only when that key activity is failing. Therefore, attribute measures can be used effectively in such areas.

For continuous improvement, use variable measures. Examples of variable measures include quality measures and time measures that motivate people to continuously decrease the time in steps or within processes. Variable measures also focus on those activities that may not be under control.

During this fifth step, the team must also determine whether the performance measure is quantified as a count, ratio, percentage, or currency amount. In process performance measures, one generally wants to focus on numbers and on whether things are achieved, i.e., attribute performance measures. Variable performance measures in the process performance measurement area often are time-driven performance measures. Using ratios and percentages yields interesting numbers, but problems can remain hidden. In fact, the aggregation of process performance measures is nonvalue-added. However, the aggregation of output performance measures may have value to management.

Sixth, **validate the process performance measures.** Because key activities and process performance measures are developed by cross-functional teams, it is important that everyone

*The process
performance measures
must be validated by
the people within
the process, or the
measures will not serve
to motivate anyone.*

understand the process and contribute input to validate the performance measures. This validation can be accomplished by posting performance measures on walls for written comments, which is a nonthreatening way to gather suggestions. Another technique is small-group meetings during which the process of determining performance measures is explained. What are the key activities that have been selected, and why? How have performance measures over those key activities been chosen? Will these measures be implemented and maintained? The process performance measures must be validated by the people within the process, or the measures will not serve to motivate anyone.

In conclusion, when determining process performance measures, be certain to relate them to the goals of the organization. Use the Matrix to guide the selection of the performance measures, and to get input and validation from everyone within the process—not just the committee that developed the performance measures.

THE CASCADING EFFECT

*Often, a process
performance measure at
one level becomes an
output performance
measure at the next
lower level.*

Often, a process performance measure at one level becomes an output performance measure at the next lower level. These performance measures cascade down the organization. The measures link the performance and goals throughout the organization, and the goals and performance measures cascade through the organization. In this way, everything is tied together from the top down.

ACTION STEPS:
SETTING AND IMPLEMENTING
PROCESS PERFORMANCE
MEASURES

Following are the steps for setting and
implementing process performance measures:

1. **Determine what the people in the process
   should focus on.** Review the goals of the
   organization, and make certain that they
   remain the driving force for determining
   the process performance measures.
2. **Determine the categories of measurement**
   by using the Matrix.
3. **Select within the Matrix the types
   of performance measures that support
   the goals.**
4. **Determine what to measure and how to
   measure it.**
5. **Determine whether the measure will be
   an attribute or a variable measure.**
6. **Validate the process performance measures.**

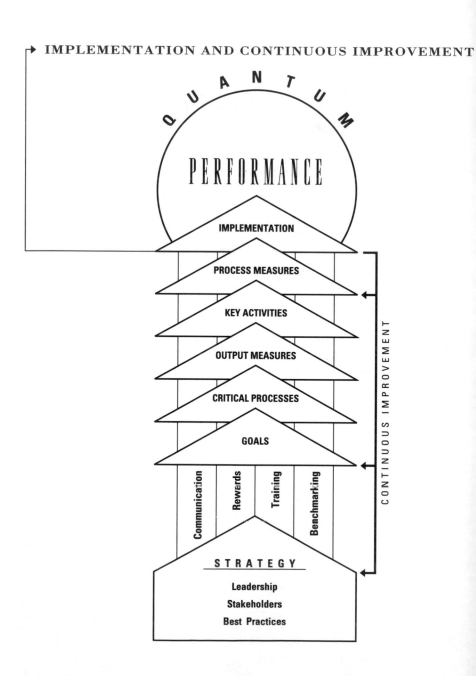

IMPLEMENTATION AND CONTINUOUS IMPROVEMENT

QUANTUM

PERFORMANCE

IMPLEMENTATION

PROCESS MEASURES

KEY ACTIVITIES

OUTPUT MEASURES

CRITICAL PROCESSES

GOALS

Communication Rewards Training Benchmarking

S T R A T E G Y

Leadership

Stakeholders

Best Practices

CONTINUOUS IMPROVEMENT

IMPLEMENTATION AND CONTINUOUS IMPROVEMENT

■ **DEFINITION**

The key to implementation is a six step process that moves from the development and validation of reporting protocol to the revision and continuous improvement of performance measures.

● **BENEFITS**

Implementation must include the people to be measured in the development process to ensure that the new measures are acceptable, reliable, and focused.

▲ **RISKS**

Without "good" implementation, change is impossible. Implementation requires feedback from every level so that strategy, goals, and process measures can be continuously improved.

With the process performance measures determined, management understands the customer wants, the output performance measures, and the process. Management also understands the key activities and the performance measures that monitor those activities and motivate people. The next step is implementation and continuous improvement.

There are five reasons why implementation can be a problem:

First, those affected by the performance measures—the people in the process—**don't think that the selected measures are important.** Perhaps they have not been involved in the development process, so they have no pride of ownership in the performance measures. Additionally, the people in the process may not understand the big picture. Even if they understand their own individual processes, they may not understand the strategy or the goals of the organization or the customer wants. Without that knowledge and understanding, it's very difficult for them to understand why the selected performance measures are important.

Second, **performance measures can be unreliable** because they do not measure what they are intended to measure or because the data that is being measured is faulty, making the performance measures untrustworthy.

One example of an unreliable performance measure is labor efficiency reporting. It is easy for the workers on the line or their supervisors to manipulate daily labor efficiency reports, either by letting bad-quality products through or by producing too much of a product, which allows individuals or the department to earn additional labor hours.

Monthly financial statements of organizations are a second example of unreliable information. Organizations can manipulate the monthly financial statements by shipping product, including incomplete or low-quality product, and recording it as sales to meet monthly sales goals. The product is returned the next month, but the sales and financial information itself is manipulated on a monthly basis and is, therefore, unreliable.

Another unreliable performance measurement is found in financial institutions. Sometimes loans are made current simply by renewing the note as opposed to actually collecting the past-due balance. The information—and therefore the performance measure—is unreliable. It's not measuring what it's supposed to measure.

Third, **performance measures are often used to criticize people rather than improve the process.** For example, in some large companies, telephone operators are measured by the length of time they spend on each call. They are limited to only a few seconds with each customer. By doing their job properly—that is, serving the customer— they exceed that time limit. Instead of being rewarded, they are criticized for not performing up to the performance measure. The measurement is focused on criticizing the person, as opposed to improving the process.

Another example of performance measures focusing on people instead of processes is in sales. Selling is usually a team effort, yet sales measures focus on the point person, not on the process itself. Many companies are moving away from having commissioned salespeople because they recognize that selling is a team effort and that performance measures focused on individuals are demotivating.

Fourth, **people do not need performance measures to perform the tasks they are required to do.** Many performance measures are unnecessary exercises that tend to irritate the persons collecting the information instead of helping them manage or continuously improve the process. There are many examples in organizations of people spending more time collecting data for measures than they spend with customers. Studies show cases where a sales force spends 90 percent of its time on bureaucratic tasks and 10 percent with the customer, as opposed to 90 percent with the customer and 10 percent on necessary paperwork. Performance measures that drive this type of activity do not help serve customers. They only interfere with operations and demotivate people.

Fifth, **initial enthusiasm related to changing performance measures may cause people to think that more is better.** Once people agree that their traditional performance measures are not appropriate, they "get religion" and go out and develop 30 or 40 or 50 performance measures. Such initial enthusiasm results in too many performance measures and a lack of focus. This enthusiasm, usually felt by top management, is viewed by the people in the process as something that will go away if ignored—as just another fad. When there are so many performance measures that everything is being measured, people are overwhelmed and don't do anything.

Given the importance of implementation—and the many reasons why efforts fail—how does one take the information generated through the process and use it properly, while also ensuring that management gets the right information to manage resources?

The key to implementation is a six-step process of performance measure implementation:

1. Develop and validate the reporting protocol.
2. Obtain management sign-off.
3. Present the implementation plan to the people in the process.
4. Start measuring and reporting.
5. Assess the effectiveness of the measures.
6. Revise and continuously improve the performance measurements.

Let's look at each of these steps individually.

STEP 1. REPORTING PROTOCOL
In this step, the team developing the process performance measures and the reporting

The key to implementation is a six-step process of performance measure implementation.

The people in the process should validate the reporting protocol.

protocol asks the people within the process to validate the reporting protocol. The reporting protocol really answers five questions:

Question 1: Who is responsible for collecting and reporting the performance measures? Since the implementation process looks at both output and process performance measures, the person in charge is responsible for collecting and reporting the output performance information. The person responsible for collecting and reporting on the process performance measure is the one responsible for that key activity in the process.

Question 2: What is being reported? Both output performance measures and process performance measures should be reported within the context of the goals, Best Practices, or targets of the organization.

Question 3: When and how often should the performance measures be reported? The performance measures should be reported within the decision response time frame. In other words, process performance measures should be reported after each occurrence so that the next time the activity takes place, it can be improved.

However, management cannot influence output performance measures as rapidly. Therefore, the information is not needed as quickly. Output measures can be reported to top management daily, weekly, or even monthly, depending on the decision response time frame. From a corporate or organizational standpoint, output performance measures are usually reported monthly because of the nature of the performance measures and the length of time required to change or respond to them.

Question 4: How is the information reported? The information should be reported in a method that is easy to use and easy to review by those affected by the performance measures. For example, process performance measures should be displayed visually within the process where they can be seen by everyone within the process. Output performance measures, since they are being used by the management of the process and by the organization, should be user-friendly— for example, graphical reports. It is important that performance measures be used—not buried in stacks of reports. Therefore, graphical representation often is best for both process and output performance measures. The seven productivity tools discussed in Chapter 8 have been used successfully to graphically represent performance measurement information.

Question 5: To whom is the information reported? The answer: Whoever **needs** to know the information should receive it—not whoever **wants** to know it. Significantly fewer people **need** to know information. From a process performance measurement standpoint, these are the people within the process, **not** management. Therefore, it's not necessary to report process performance measures to management. However, output performance measures

It is important that performance measures be used—not buried in stacks of reports.

are the responsibility of management since these measures are used to control resources. But they need not necessarily be available to the people within a process except for review.

These are the five questions that have to be answered in developing the reporting protocol. The people in the process must validate this reporting protocol. Their input is essential for buy-in and motivation. The answers to these questions should not be developed in a vacuum. Members of management and the people in the process must be involved in developing the reporting protocol.

STEP 2. MANAGEMENT SIGN-OFF

Management should sign off on the output performance measures, on how often they review the elements of the reporting protocol, and on the nature of both process and output performance measures.

Performance measures should cascade down the organization and be tied to its strategies and goals. Just as it is important for the output and process performance measures to be developed by the people within the process, so must the reporting protocol. Management should sign off on the output performance measures, on how often they review the elements of the reporting protocol, and on the nature of both process and output performance measures. Many of the unnecessary reports in companies today started from a request for information from management that has been institutionalized. It's not that management shouldn't get information. But the information should be based on a verified need, not just on what was done before.

STEP 3. PRESENTING THE PLAN

Throughout the entire process of identifying
and implementing performance measures,
communication about project status should
be continued. It is important to bring everyone
in the process up to date on progress and results
of implementing the Quantum Performance
Measurement Model.

A series of presentations should start with the
strategy of the organization, how the strategy
is decomposed into goals, and how those goals
affect the individual processes as part of the
output performance measures. The process
and the key activities validated should be
reviewed by the group. Finally, the reporting
protocol that has just been developed and
validated should be presented to the group,
along with the implementation plan.
These meetings are important to ensure
that the people involved in the process
as well as the people involved in developing,
implementing, and using the performance
measures understand the big picture.

STEP 4. MEASURING AND REPORTING

Now that the people within the process have
heard and commented on the implementation
plan, the fourth step is measuring and reporting
the performance measures. This is where one
performs, captures, and uses both process and
output performance measures.

Throughout the entire process of identifying and implementing performance measures, it is important to bring everyone in the process up to date on progress and results.

To identify and analyze problems continuously, use the seven productivity tools discussed in Chapter 8.

STEP 5. ASSESSING EFFECTIVENESS

Assessing the effectiveness of performance measures should be done to ensure that the measures selected, both process and output, are meeting their goals.

Assessing the effectiveness of these measures probably should be done approximately three to six months after the implementation has started to ensure that the performance measures selected, both process and output, are meeting their goals— to report the outputs of a process, to continuously improve the process, and to motivate the people within the process.

STEP 6. CONTINUOUS IMPROVEMENT

The final step in the implementation process is to continuously revise and improve the performance measures. Often it is necessary to adjust the performance measures because the team does not have a clear understanding of what the key activities are or what performance measures are necessary to monitor and control them.

This is an ongoing task of systematically monitoring to ensure that the key activities remain key activities, that the performance measures selected to monitor those key activities are proper performance measures, and that the output performance measures still focus on customer wants, the goals of the organization, and the strategies of the company. This systematic revision and continuous improvement is done on a yearly basis by revisiting the process and the goals and strategies of the organization.

Through the Quantum Performance Measurement Model, management gets feedback from the implementation and use of performance measures. This feedback is used by management to recalibrate the organization's strategy, goals, and process measures.

Strategy: As the processes or outputs improve or change, the strategy also may change. For example, if the performance measures in manufacturing help the company decrease the lot size, the company's sales strategy and target markets may change. If the company, through the use of performance measures, is able to reduce the cycle time of taking and acting on a customer order, it can change its sales strategies to offer customers different incentives, such as fast shipment or fast response time, in order to increase its market or to compete against different competitors. The performance measures not only impact the process, but they also allow management to change outputs.

Goals: As processes continuously improve and management uses output performance measures to monitor the consumption of resources and to manage the business, goals can change. Strategy may not change, but goals will continuously aim higher.

Process Measures: As processes improve, the process measures and key activities should be reassessed.

Feedback from the implementation and use of performance measures is used by management to recalibrate the organization's strategy, goals, and process measures.

Therefore, the information provided by monitoring performance measures does three things. First, it impacts the strategy, output, and processes of an organization, since this feedback focuses on the continuous improvement of the process. Second, the information motivates the people within the process. Third, the information can be used by management to control the resources of the process.

ORGANIZING THE TEAM

Teams must be organized to develop and implement a new performance measurement system for the organization.

Several teams must be organized to use the Quantum Performance Measurement Model to develop and implement a new performance measurement system for the organization. They include a Steering Team and several Performance Measurement Teams.

The Steering Team should be made up of the top management of the organization and should include the Chief Executive Officer, Chief Financial Officer, and functional area executives. One Steering Team member should be selected as the Steering Team Leader. This person must dedicate a minimum of 20 percent of his or her time to leading the performance measurement effort.

The Steering Team is responsible for leading and coordinating the effort throughout the organization.

The Steering Team is responsible for leading and coordinating the effort throughout the organization. Team members must revisit and/or develop the organization's vision and strategy, identify performance goals and measures, and appropriately use the four enablers—

communication, training, rewards, and benchmarking—to create awareness, buy-in, and ownership of the new performance measurement system among all employees.

Figure 10.2 shows some of the activities that need to be performed and who is responsible for each.

The Steering Team then identifies the organization's critical processes and organizes cross-functional Performance Measurement Teams to develop output measures and complete the remaining activities in the Quantum Performance Measurement Model. Although each Performance Measurement Team is responsible for the design and implementation of output and process performance measures for its process, it is the Steering Team's responsibility to ensure that all Performance Measurement Teams are provided the appropriate resources and training. The Steering Team must also ensure that all performance measures implemented are aligned with one another throughout the organization.

Each Performance Measurement Team is responsible for the design and implementation of output and process performance measures for its process.

If the Quantum Performance Measurement Model is implemented only on the process level, the Performance Measurement Teams must attempt to align the performance measures on the process level with those on the organization level. Although it is possible to use the Model for the process level only, suboptimization may occur.

The Quantum Performance Measurement Model can be used on the people level as well.

FIGURE 10.2
DIVISION OF RESPONSIBILITY
Adapted from Joseph R. Jablonski (1991). Used with the permission
of Joseph Jablonski and the Technical Management Consortium.

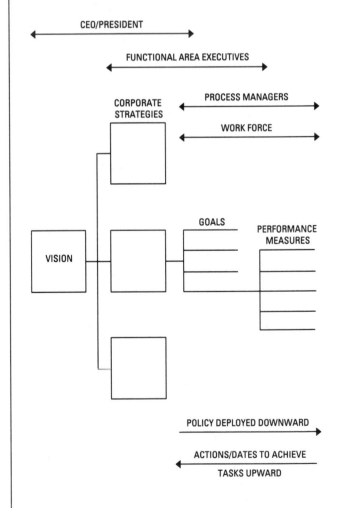

Following are some of the critical activities and performance measures on this level that could be tracked on a daily or weekly basis:

- Number of times late for a meeting
- Number of pieces of paper handled more than once
- Time spent searching for something that has been misplaced or lost
- Number of phone calls not returned on the same day

Although the final step of the Quantum Performance Measurement Model is Implementation and Continuous Improvement, the Steering and Performance Measurement Teams should begin the process with the mindset of implementation and continuous improvement. The team should keep in mind that the measures developed must be used by the people to continuously improve processes and by management to innovate new processes. Figure 10.3 shows how continuous improvement results in gradual performance improvement, while breakaway thinking by management results in process innovations and radical increases in process improvement. Although everyone in the organization can engage in breakaway thinking to innovate processes, management is responsible for providing the resources to reengineer these processes.

The objective of implementing a balanced set of performance measures is not to make "busy

Steering and Performance Measurement Teams should begin the process with the mindset of implementation and continuous improvement.

FIGURE 10.3
**CONTINUOUS IMPROVEMENT AND
PROCESS INNOVATION**

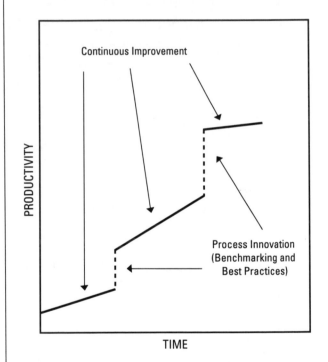

work" for people but rather to help an organization achieve Quantum Performance. Quantum Performance is that level of achievement that optimizes the organization's value and service to its stakeholders. It is important to remember that this objective is a never-ending target. Because the stakeholders of an organization have changing and, in fact, increasing expectations, the objective of Quantum Performance cannot be achieved. This is why the feedback loops are critically important, not only in implementation but also in continually focusing on the changes that are necessary in the organization.

The development of cost, quality, and time performance measures and the implementation of this family of performance measures allow a company to optimize its value and service. The feedback loops give management and the people in the processes the facts they need to continuously improve their strategy, their goals, and the processes.

The information received through the feedback loops allows management and the people in the processes to see the results of their actions. This allows them to continuously change to meet the changing expectations of the stakeholders.

The information received through the feedback loops allows management and the people in the processes to see the results of their actions and to continuously change to meet the changing expectations of the stakeholders.

ACTION STEPS: IMPLEMENTATION AND CONTINUOUS IMPROVEMENT

Following are the steps for implementation and continuous improvement.

1. Validate the reporting protocol.
2. Obtain management sign-off on:

   - The output measures
   - How often the information is needed
   - Why certain information is needed

3. Present the performance measurements to all impacted stakeholders.
4. Capture, monitor and analyze, and report the performance measures.
5. Assess the effectiveness of the implemented measures.
6. Continuously revise and improve the performance measures.

VITAL SIGNS

THE FOLLOWING

EXAMPLE

ILLUSTRATES

THE USE OF

THE QUANTUM

PERFORMANCE

MEASUREMENT

MATRIX AND MODEL.

11

QUANTUM PERFORMANCE MATRIX AND MODEL APPLICATION

It is often helpful to demonstrate performance measure concepts through the use of a case study. The following example illustrates the use of the Quantum Performance Measurement Matrix and Model. The company is a $400-million manufacturer of consumer products.

Like most companies in this environment, the company is dealing with increased competition, both domestic and foreign. In fact, many of the company's domestic competitors have moved their manufacturing operations to countries with lower labor rates. At the same time, some foreign competitors have moved part of their assembly operations to the United States to be closer to the market and to decrease the time in the delivery process to their U.S. customers.

In addition, the company is facing a market that is becoming more sophisticated because of the increased competition and an ever-changing system of government regulations.

DRIVERS

The first step in developing, implementing, and using performance measures is the development of a corporate strategy that uses the input of the leadership of the organization, the expectations of the various stakeholder groups, and Best Practices. These are the drivers of the Quantum Performance Measurement Model. See Figure 11.1.

LEADERSHIP

Top management is responsible for prioritizing and balancing the demands of the stakeholders, prioritizing and allocating the scarce resources of the organization, and being involved in development, implementation, and use of performance measures. They form a Steering Team to lead and manage the performance measurement process. In turn, they select a Performance Measurement Team to develop and implement the appropriate performance measures.

STAKEHOLDERS

The company has three groups of stakeholders: **customers, shareholders,** and **employees.** The company has segmented its customer group and, through research, determined that the **customers** want new products with new features. The **shareholders** want continued and increased profitability, increasing return on investment, and a growing company. The **employees** want job security and increased job satisfaction.

FIGURE 11.1
QUANTUM PERFORMANCE
MEASUREMENT MODEL

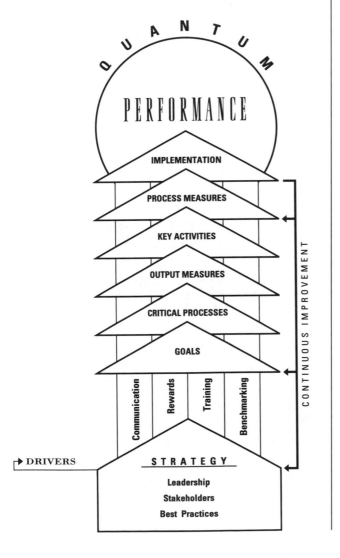

BEST PRACTICES

The company realizes that there are more efficient and effective ways of performing many of its processes. Management wants to decrease the learning curve in many of these process improvement areas. As part of the strategic planning process, the company is looking to the competition and to other industries to understand and use "Best Practices."

STRATEGY

With input from leadership, stakeholders, and Best Practices, the company develops a corporate strategy. One component of that strategy is to maintain customer loyalty. Management has determined, through cross-industry research, that it's more profitable to have loyal customers than to try to replace lost customers. They also have debated about the best way of maintaining customer loyalty: Either lower the price of the product, or introduce more products that satisfy unmet customer wants.

Customer research supports the new product approach. If the company can bring out new products with more features, faster, this will help capture customer loyalty. Top management of the organization has decided on the new product development strategy, which will cause the Performance Measurement Team to focus on "new product development" as a **critical process**— a process to improve, control, and monitor continuously with new performance measures.

FIGURE 11.2
QUANTUM PERFORMANCE
MEASUREMENT MODEL

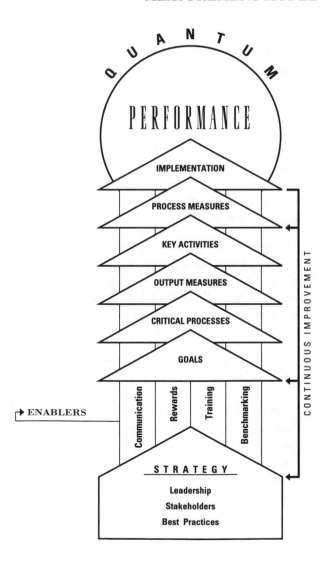

ENABLERS

Understanding the importance of the enablers
and using input of associates from all levels
and departments, management develops
a plan for communication, rewards, training,
and benchmarking.

COMMUNICATION

This plan includes a one-hour companywide meeting
to explain to all associates why the company needs
to develop a new performance measurement system.
Associates are then asked to go back to their work
areas to ask further questions of their bosses and to
develop of list of questions and concerns that need
to be addressed by top management.

The progress and status of performance measures
is to be an agenda item of every meeting of
members of top management. Top management
agrees that if they all do this, others will realize
how important these measures are to the
organization. The company newsletter will
have a column in each issue on the performance
measurement system.

REWARDS

Management decides not to tie monetary pay
to changed behavior. They focus instead on
nonmonetary rewards for teams that meet and
exceed performance targets and/or make the most
improvement. This would include congratulatory
notes, posted pictures of the team, and other
recognition techniques.

FIGURE 11.3
QUANTUM PERFORMANCE
MEASUREMENT MODEL

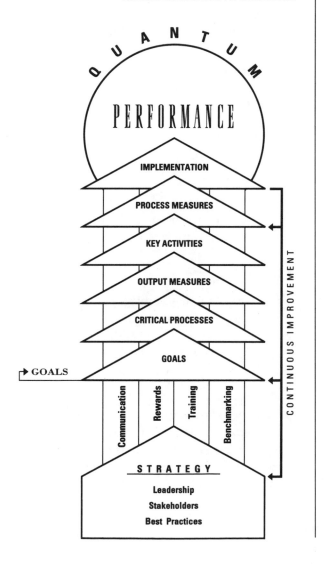

223

TRAINING

The courses listed below are offered to any associate in the organization who feels that he or she will benefit from the skills and concepts taught in the following areas:

- Process mapping
- Problem solving
- The seven planning and management tools
- Performance measurement and quantum performance
- Managers and leaders: From controllers to coaches

BENCHMARKING

Finally, areas to benchmark, both inside and outside the company, are determined.

GOALS

The company now has a strategy of maintaining customer loyalty through rapid product introduction. The leadership of the organization must set goals that drive and link to this strategy. The company then develops three goals:

- The first goal is to get products to market (from concept to first product in the marketplace) 50 percent faster over the next two years.
- The second goal is to develop two new products per year that have market acceptance.
- The third goal is to have 25 percent of the company's profits come from new products in two years.

FIGURE 11.4
QUANTUM PERFORMANCE
MEASUREMENT MODEL

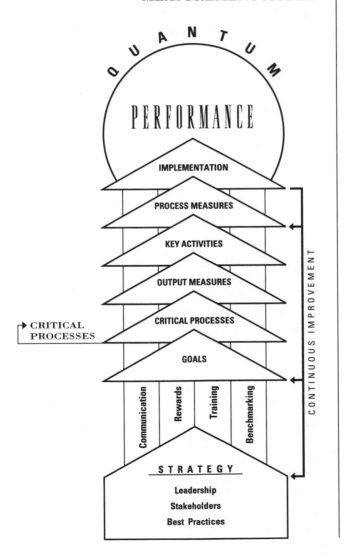

Interestingly, the Performance Measurement Team has balanced the goals of **time** (speed to market), **quality** (two new products demanded by the customers), and **cost** (25 percent of revenues coming from new products in the next two years).

CRITICAL PROCESSES

The first step in identifying the critical processes is to identify the major processes of the organization. The Performance Measurement Team starts with the customer—with an understanding of what the customer receives from the organization— and then works backwards to the organization. This distinguishes the primary, support, and management processes.

In this case, the processes identified by the team include determining customer needs and wants, measuring customer satisfaction, monitoring the external environment, developing and setting organizational goals, planning and acquiring necessary resources and inputs into the processes, marketing and selling to customers, billing customers, planning and management, and developing new products.

The Performance Measurement Team then categorizes these as primary, support, or management processes. This enables the company to prioritize the allocation of its scarce resources and improve its processes. A primary process— one that touches the customer—is new product development. A support process is financial

FIGURE 11.5
QUANTUM PERFORMANCE
MEASUREMENT MODEL

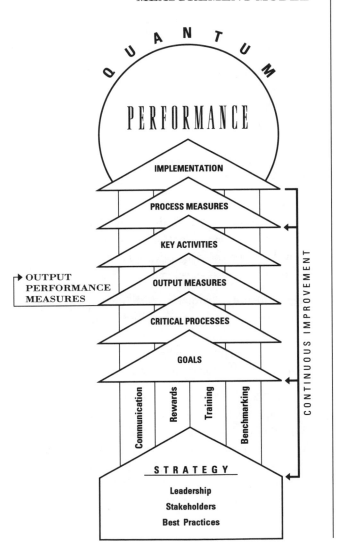

reporting. A management process is measuring customer satisfaction.

The next step for the Performance Measurement Team is to identify the **critical processes** by using the goals of the organization as criteria. Two goals, "get products to market 50 percent faster over the next two years" and "develop two new products a year that have market acceptance," are directly related to the new product development process.

OUTPUT PERFORMANCE MEASURES

The next step in the Quantum Performance Measurement Model is the design and development of output performance measures. For this case, we will develop the output performance measures for the new product development process.

Step 1: Identify customers (both internal and external). For this company, the internal customers of new product development are the people in the production and purchasing processes. The external customers are the buyers of the products.

Step 2: Identify and understand customers' expectations of the process. Using structured brainstorming techniques, the company identifies customer expectations. Production wants no engineering change notices, long production runs, and products that have been designed for manufacturability—ones that require no new machinery or tooling and, therefore, incur no additional training costs. Purchasing wants large lot sizes, long order lead times so that it can order ahead of time and get large discounts, and strong vendor relationships (and no new vendors). The external customers—the buyers of the products—want products with features they define. They also want products that are dependable and competitively priced.

Step 3: Filter and prioritize customers' expectations based on the goals of the organization. The Performance Measurement Team starts by setting output performance measures on the most important, critical elements of the process. The goals, derived from the strategies of the company, are used to prioritize the expectations of the customers. In this case, the strategies are to increase speed to market, develop two new products a year, and obtain 25 percent of profits from new products. The goals are to make a product that customers want and that is designed for manufacturability, and to devise a new product development process that is very quick. In addition, the new product development process should be done at a reasonable cost.

Step 4: Select output performance measures. After identifying and prioritizing customer expectations, the Performance Measurement Team uses the criteria of cost, quality and time to develop performance measures. The team uses the Matrix as a guide in the selection process. A good performance measure would be the cycle time of product development. A flexibility performance measure for manufacturability would be the number of parts in the product or the number of vendors required to supply materials. The cost performance measure would be the budget for new product development. To measure whether the product is desired, an output performance measure would be asking customers, "Would you buy the product?" among other product- and service-specific questions in focus groups or through surveys.

Step 5: Set targets. Since new product development is a primary process—it touches the customer—the Performance Measurement Team bases targets on world-class standards for new product development. The team researches its own industry and other industries to determine these world-class targets for budgets, cycle time, flexibility, and desirability.

KEY ACTIVITIES

The next step in the Model is to identify key activities in the new product development process. First, the team defines the process, where it starts and stops, and the inputs and outputs to the process.

Second, the team documents the process. This is done by interviewing the people familiar with the process—not only people working in the process, but those external to it, including internal and external customers and suppliers. This information and the results of the interviews are often documented on a process map. The purpose of the process map is to visually represent the activities of

FIGURE 11.6
QUANTUM PERFORMANCE
MEASUREMENT MODEL

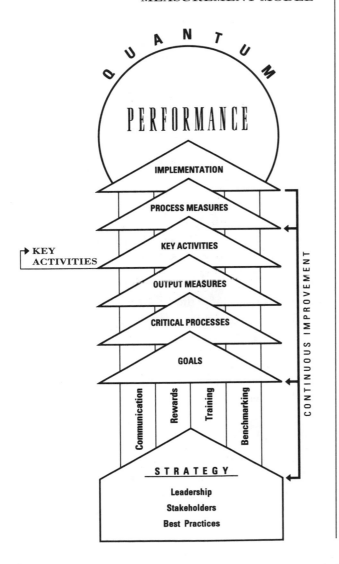

the process. This helps people to focus on what's important and to highlight waste in the process.

Third, the team identifies key activities in the process. A key activity is a step critical to the process and the output. As a rule of thumb, there should be no more than six key activities in a process. In the new product development process, the team identifies four key activities: conceptual design, product design, prototyping, and target costing.

PROCESS PERFORMANCE MEASURES

The next step in the Quantum Performance Measurement Model is to design process performance measures for each key activity. In this example, we'll look at the conceptual design activity.

First, the Performance Measurement Team examines the goals of the organization. The goals of the new company focus are speed, market acceptance, and profits.

The second step the Performance Measurement Team performs is to use the Quantum Performance Measurement Matrix and the cost, quality, and time criteria as a guide in the selection of the process performance measures.

Third, the team determines **what** and **how** to measure. Looking at the **process** and its key activities, the team identifies several process performance measures. One measure is early supplier involvement. This can be measured

FIGURE 11.7
**QUANTUM PERFORMANCE
MEASUREMENT MODEL**

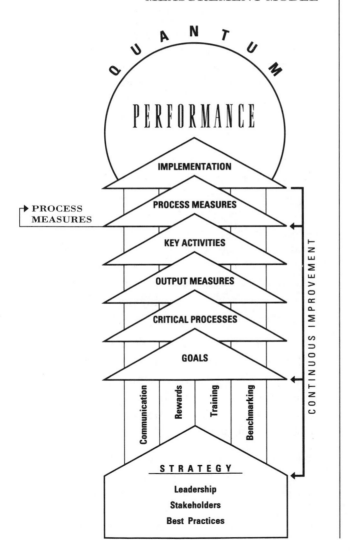

by having suppliers involved by a specific date—for instance, by the second meeting of the new product development team. This is both an attribute (yes or no) measure and a quality measure. In addition, the team wants cross-functional input. This is a quality measure at the process level and is another attribute measure. The team lists all the departments that should have input and ensures that all departments are represented at the right time, using Best Practices in new product development.

Another performance measure the team selects is the use of design standards. This is, again, a quality measure: conformance. The team wants process performance measures to focus on time—flexibility—and the number of common parts in the product design. These are "variable measures." Process performance measures will also track velocity, or the number of steps required in the manufacturing process to produce the product. This is another variable performance measure.

At the same time, the team needs people performance measures for quality. The team should consider measuring competency and resilience. Competency is whether the right people are involved in the process, and resilience is the number of skills they have.

Fourth, the Performance Measurement Team validates these process performance measures. Process performance measures are validated by the people in the process. They are asked whether the performance measures give them control

FIGURE 11.8
QUANTUM PERFORMANCE
MEASUREMENT MODEL

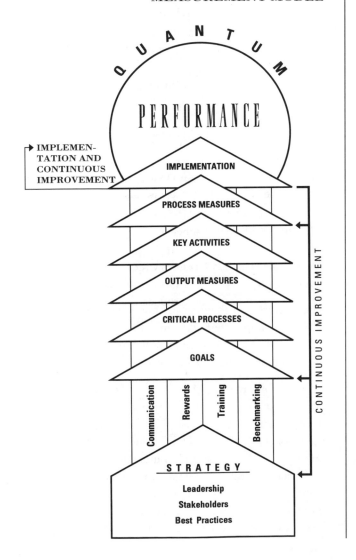

over the process and whether the measures allow them to continuously improve the process.

Fifth, the Performance Measurement Team determines whether the performance measures are attribute or variable. Measurement is easier with attribute measures: with a simple "yes" or "no" answer. Variable performance measures are used to continuously improve the process or to elicit the reasons for a "no" attribute measure. In this case, the attribute measures include early supplier involvement, cross-functional inputs, and the use of standards. The variable measures include the use of common parts, the number of steps in the manufacturing process, and the right people with the right skills.

IMPLEMENTATION AND CONTINUOUS IMPROVEMENT

The final step for the Performance Measurement Team is to implement and continuously improve. The team takes a four-step approach in the implementation process.

First, the Performance Measurement Team develops and validates the reporting protocol by asking questions such as: "Who's responsible for the reporting?" "What's the best way to report?" "When?" and "How often?" In this case, the output performance measures will be reported to top management. Because of the importance of this process, all the output performance measures will be on the same report and, if possible, graphically

FIGURE 11.9
PERFORMANCE MEASURES
DEPLOYMENT

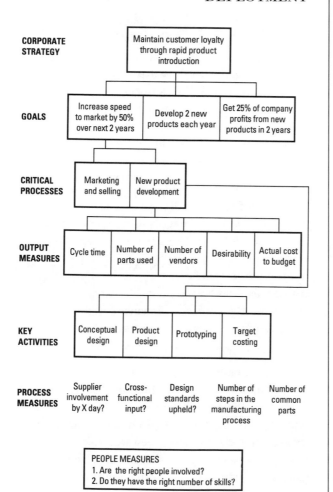

represented. The report will include the actual current performance, historical trends, projected activity in the near future, and performance measures compared to world-class benchmarks.

The process performance measures stay within the process. These measures are very important to the people within the process as a way to continuously control and improve the process. But the measures need not be reported to management on a periodic basis. The process performance measures are shown on display boards as opposed to written reports.

The second step in implementation is to gain management sign-off. All the performance measures tie to the management strategy of rapid product development (with the goals of speed to market, two new products a year, and 25 percent of the profits coming from new products). Also, management has been involved from the beginning of the process. Therefore, there's no barrier to management sign-off.

Third, the Performance Measurement Team presents the plan to the people in the process. Because all the people have been involved throughout the process, they know what's going on. At this point, the team needs to communicate that the final conclusions were based on all their inputs, to answer their questions, and to bring closure to the process.

Fourth, the company starts measuring and reporting. There should be few barriers because the people in the process have been involved

throughout. They have also been trained
in these new skills, and the company has a
communication strategy in which "listening"
is as important as "broadcasting."

The measuring and reporting start immediately.
The company gives the new performance
measures time to work. As part of their
continuous improvement, in six months, the
Performance Measurement Team will evaluate
the measures and assess their effectiveness.
The team will revise the measures if the
measures are not helping management focus
on the goals of the organization or helping
the people continuously improve the process.

The Performance Measurement Team uses
Figure 11.9 to help ensure that the measures
that have been implemented focus on the right
things and that old measures are in alignment.

This figure will be especially helpful to the
company after all three goals are achieved.
It helps to rededicate the company to achieving
the "impossible" goal of Quantum Performance.

REFERENCES AND SUGGESTED READING

Akao, Yoji (1988). *Quality Function Deployment: Integrating Customer Requirements Into Product Design*, Cambridge, MA: Productivity Press.

American National Standard: Quality Systems—Model for Quality Assurance in Design/Development, Production, Installation, and Servicing (1987). Milwaukee, WI: American Society for Quality Control.

ANSI/ASQC Q90-1987 Series (1987). Milwaukee, WI: ASQC.

Barker, Joel Arthur (1992). *Future Edge*. New York: William Morrow and Company, Inc.

Beer, Michael, Eisenstat, Russell A., and Spector, Bert (1990). "Why Change Programs Don't Produce Change." *Harvard Business Review*, November-December 1990, Vol. 68, No. 6, pp. 158-166.

Blueprints for Service Quality: The Federal Express Approach (1991). New York: AMA Membership Publication Division.

Brassard, Michael (1988). *The Memory Jogger™: A Pocket Guide of Tools for Continuous Improvement*. Methuen, MA: GOAL/QPC (508) 685-3900.

Brassard, Michael (1989). *The Memory Jogger Plus+™*. Methuen, MA: GOAL/QPC (508) 685-3900.

Camp, Robert C. (1989). *Benchmarking*. Milwaukee, WI: ASQC Quality Press.

Chappell, Lindsay (1992). "Plant Floor Is Fertile Soil for Ideas." *Automotive News*, April 27, 1992, p. 4.

Deming, Dr. W. Edwards (1991). Meeting and discussion with Steven M. Hronec. Cincinnati.

Gery, Gloria J. (1991). *Electronic Performance Support Systems: How and Why to Remake the Workplace Through the Strategic Application of Technology*. Boston: Weingarten Publications, Inc.

Gryna, Frank M. and Juran, Joseph M. (1989). *Juran on Leadership for Quality: An Executive Handbook*. New York: The Free Press.

Hankinson, Holbrook, and Lloyd, Shelley P. (1992). Change Management. In Barry J. Brinker (Ed.), *Handbook of Cost Management* (pp. E2-1 - E2-22). Boston: Warren, Gorham & Lamont.

Hronec, Steven M., and Hunt, Steven K. (1992). Quality and Cost Management. In Barry J. Brinker (Ed.), *Handbook of Cost Management* (pp. A1-1 - A1-34). Boston: Warren, Gorham & Lamont.

Jablonski, Joseph R. (1991). *Implementing Total Quality Management: An Overview*. Albuquerque, NM: Technical Management Consortium.

Juran, Joseph M. (1992). *Juran On Quality By Design: The New Steps for Planning Quality into Goods and Services*. New York: The Free Press.

1992 Award Criteria: Malcolm Baldrige National Quality Award. Milwaukee, WI: American Society for Quality Control.

Orsburn, Jack D., Moran, Linda, Musselwhite, Ed, and Zenger, John H. (1990). *Self-Directed Work Teams: The New American Challenge*. Homewood, IL: Business One Irwin.

Pascarella, Perry (1987). "Resistance to Change: It Can Be a Plus." *Industry Week,* July 27, 1987, Vol. 236, No. 14, pp. 45-47.

Peters, Thomas (1987). *Passion for Customers* (video). Schaumburg, IL: Video Publishing House.

Reddy, N. Mohan (1991). "Designing Product Value in Industrial Markets." *Management Decision,* Vol. 29, Issue 1, pp. 14-19.

Rummler, Geary, and Brache, Alan P. (1990). *Improving Performance: How to Manage the White Space in the Organizational Chart.* San Francisco: Jossey-Bass Publishers.

Rummler, Geary (1992). Meetings and discussions with Steven M. Hronec. Los Angeles.

Schlesinger, Leonard A., and Heskett, James L. (1991). "The Service-Driven Service Company." *Harvard Business Review,* September-October 1991, Vol. 69, pp. 71-81.

Schlesinger, Leonard A., and Heskett, James L. (1991). "Leonard A. Schlesinger and James L. Heskett Respond." In "How Does Service Drive the Service Company?" *Harvard Business Review,* November-December 1991, Vol. 69, pp. 148-149.

Scott, Cynthia D., and Jaffe, Dennis T. (1988). "Survive and Thrive in Times of Change." *Training and Development Journal,* April 1988, Vol. 42, No. 4, pp. 25-27.

Taylor, Frederick W. (1911). The Principles of Scientific Management. New York: Harper and Brothers.

"Teamwork Overhauls GM's Van Nuys Plant" (1987). *The Sacramento Bee,* June 1, 1987, p. D1.

Van Hull, Peter (1992). Meeting and discussion with Steven M. Hronec. St. Charles, IL.

Zeithaml, Valerie A., Parasuraman, A., and Berry, Leonard L. (1990). *Delivering Quality Service.* New York: The Free Press.

Zenger, John (1992). "Laying the Foundation for Quality Improvement." *Human Side of Quality Conference,* Washington, D.C., September 14, 1992.